A M E R I C A N   T R A I L S

CATTLE TRAILS
"Git Along Little Dogies..."

AMERICAN TRAILS

CATTLE TRAILS
"Git Along Little Dogies..."

KATHY PELTA

RSVP

RAINTREE
STECK-VAUGHN
PUBLISHERS
The Steck-Vaughn Company

Austin, Texas

Published by Raintree Steck-Vaughn Publishers, an imprint of Steck-Vaughn Company

Raintree Steck-Vaughn Publishers Staff
Publishing Director: Walter Kossmann   Project Manager: Lyda Guz
Editor: Shirley Shalit   Electronic Production: Scott Melcer
Photo Editor: Margie Foster

Library of Congress Cataloging-in-Publication Data
Pelta, Kathy.
    Cattle trails : "get along little dogies" / by Kathy Pelta.
       p.   cm.– (American trails)
    Includes bibliographical references and index.
    Summary: Describes the history and customs of life along the American cattle trails.
    ISBN 0-8172-4073-X
    1. Cattle trails – West (U.S.) – Juvenile literature.   2. Frontier and pioneer life –
West (U.S.) – Juvenile literature.   3. Cattle trails – United States – Juvenile literature.
4. Frontier and pioneer life – United States – Juvenile literature. [1. Cattle trails –
History. 2. West (U.S.) – History. 3. Frontier and pioneer life – West (U.S.)
4. Cowboys.] I. Title. II. Series: Pelta, Kathy. American trails.
F596.P44 1997
978 – dc21   96-36876
                                            CIP   AC

Printed and bound in the United States
1 2 3 4 5 6 7 8 9 0 LB 00 99 98 97

Acknowledgments
The author and publisher would like to thank The Caxton Printers, Ltd., Caldwell, Idaho, for permission to reprint the quote from John K. Rollinson's *Wyoming Cattle Trails* which appears on pages 80-81. The author and publisher would also like to thank the following for photos and illustrations.
Cover (inset) © Superstock, (map) The Granger Collection; p. 3 Corbis-Bettmann; pp. 6-7 Buffalo Bill Historical Center, Cody, Wyoming; p. 9 Corbis-Bettmann; p. 12 Denver Public Library, Western History Department; p. 14 Bisbee Mining & History Museum; p. 16 Wyoming Division of Cultural Resources; p. 18 The Granger Collection; p. 22 Culver Pictures; p. 27 (top right) Brown Brothers, (bottom left) Corbis-Bettmann; p. 31 Coffrin's Old West Gallery; pp. 33, 34 © Superstock; p. 35 Denver Public Library, Western History Department; p. 39 Coffrin's Old West Gallery; p. 40 Kansas State Historical Society, Topeka, Kansas; p. 43 Archives & Manuscripts Division of the Oklahoma Historical Society; p. 45 The Granger Collection; p. 47 © Aneal F. Vohra/Unicorn Stock Photos; pp. 48, 49, 50 Kansas State Historical Society, Topeka, Kansas; p. 51 © Marshall Prescott/Unicorn Stock Photos; p. 52 © Aneal F. Vohra/Unicorn Stock Photos; p. 53 The Granger Collection; p. 56 Western History Collections, University of Oklahoma Library; p. 57 Coffrin's Old West Gallery; p. 60 Kansas State Historical Society, Topeka, Kansas; p.61 Amon Carter Museum of Western Art; p. 62 Western History Collections, University of Oklahoma Library; p. 64 Courtesy Texas Highways; p. 66 Corbis-Bettmann; p. 68 Kansas State Historical Society, Topeka, Kansas; p. 70 Western History Collections, University of Oklahoma Library; p. 72 Oliver Loving by C.L. Douglas/Texas Tech University, Lubbock, Texas; p. 77 Brown Brothers; p. 82 © Steve Warble; p. 84 Brown Brothers; p. 86 Corbis-Bettmann; p. 88 © Jack Olsen.

Cartography: GeoSystems, Inc.

Contents:

North American Trails

There were trails winding through the woods and wilderness of North America long before any Europeans arrived. Some paths were those that animals took to salt licks, or to favorite water holes. Native Americans used such paths or created their own as they hunted and gathered food, traded with neighbors, and made pilgrimages to sacred sites.

The first Europeans to explore North America usually followed established trails. Sometimes, with the help of native guides, they blazed new ones. After the explorers came soldiers and missionaries, traders and trappers, and—eventually—settlers. Gradually, favorite trails were widened to accommodate oxcarts and horse-drawn wagons, then stagecoaches, and finally, motorcars. Some trails became routes for railroad lines.

The nation's trails reflected its history. In the 1500s and after, Spain claimed much of what is now the United States. Then, trails in the Southeast, the Southwest, and along the coast of what is now California linked Spanish missions, military posts, and towns.

In the 1600s, people from other countries of Europe set-

A herd of longhorn cattle on the trail.

tled on North America's eastern shores. As they moved inland, they, too, established trails. By the late 1700s, their trails reached the Mississippi River, then the western frontier of the United States.

By the mid-1800s, Americans had ventured beyond the Mississippi as they followed the Oregon Trail, the California Trail, and other trails to the Far West. These westbound travelers included adventurers, prospectors, religious groups, and homesteaders seeking better lives for their families.

As the nation grew, so did its need for food. So trails of a different sort were developed—this time for herded animals, rather than people. By the late-1800s, cattle trails crisscrossed the western half of the United States. Some stretched from Utah and Texas to California as cowboys herded their cattle west to feed beef-starved miners during the Gold Rush. Trails led north from Texas to railheads in Kansas where the cattle were loaded on trains to be shipped east. Other trails crossed the Great Plains to the Dakotas, or led into Montana as cowmen moved herds to feed hungry reservation Indians. Even the emigrants' road to Oregon of the 1840s became a cattle trail when descendants of the animals Oregon-bound pioneers had brought west were trailed to ranches east of the Rockies four decades later. This is the story of cattle, cowboys, and cowmen—and of the western trails they followed.

From Vaquero
to Buckaroo

Soon after Columbus's first voyage the Spaniards brought cattle and horses to the New World. By the late 1700s priests at the Spanish missions in California and north of the Rio Grande in what is now Texas were raising cattle to provide leather for shoes, boots, and saddles, and tallow (fat) to make candles and soap. The mission Indians learned to ride the horses and tend the tough, long-horned cattle. Called *vaqueros* (from *vaca*, the Spanish word for cow), they became skilled horsemen, able to use *la reata*—the braided rawhide rope they looped to catch a steer on the run.

Mexico—which included both California and Texas—declared itself independent from Spain in 1821 and ended the mission system. Private *rancheros*, or ranchers, took over the mission livestock. To tend the cattle the ranchers hired the vaqueros, who by then were experts at both riding and roping. The vaqueros could cut stock—ride into a herd to separate out a rancher's cattle and calves from those of his neighbors. In a flash they could rope each animal and brand it—burn the ranch symbol on its hide with a hot branding iron.

After Spanish rule ended in Mexico, families from the United States began to settle in Texas. Most brought cattle of their own—mainly British breeds with short horns. In time the British livestock mixed with the wild Spanish cattle to produce what came to be called "Texas cows," and later "Texas longhorns," because of their long curved horns. Many of these cattle wandered among thick bushes and small trees, unclaimed and unbranded.

By the time Texas broke away from Mexico in 1836, and became a state in 1845, Texans had learned to work cattle on horseback, the Mexican way. Like the Mexicans they marked their stock with brands and notched ears, then turned the cattle onto the open range to graze. The Texans adopted the vaquero's way of dressing, and some of his terms. They penned the animals in a corral. They tossed la reata—which they called a "lariat," often made with twisted hemp (plant fiber) rather than braided rawhide. They changed *el lazo* the Spanish word for rope or snare, to "lasso." The Texas herder, like the vaquero, wore a wide-brimmed sombrero (hat) to keep out the sun, and chaperras (thick leather pants that he called "chaps") to protect his legs from the scratchy underbrush. Eventually,

In this drawing by Frederic Remington, Mexican cowboys (vaqueros) are shown shoeing a horse.

Texans changed vaquero into "buckaroo," another word for cowherder, but by the time of the great cattle drives north, Texans began to call themselves "cowboys."

Catching Strays

According to the law after Texas became a republic, any stray animal that a person caught and branded belonged to that person. Some new settlers from the United States started their herds with stray "Texas cows." The problem was catching the wild Texas longhorned cattle. They hid in thickets by day, and only came out after dark to eat or drink. Their sharp sense of smell warned if humans were near.

Herders often worked at night, trapping the animals at a water hole and driving them into a pen—making sure to stay clear of the sharp horns that could gore and kill. By day, the herders used tame decoy cattle to lure the wild cattle from the brush, or they pulled the animals out by force with the help of lariat and horse. Then they tied the wild cattle to trees or "hog-tied" them—fastened their feet together. An especially unruly animal was tied to a tame work ox.

ONE

Trail Fever

From the time E. C. (Teddy Blue) Abbott went on his first cattle drive, when he was ten years old he was struck with "trail fever." All he wanted was to become a cowboy. In 1871, his father, a Nebraska settler, had taken Teddy along when he went to Texas to buy cattle for his farm. Since no rail lines ran from Nebraska to Texas, the two rode the train to New Orleans and then took a boat to the Texas coast. After buying his herd Mr. Abbott took a stagecoach to the nearest rail line and caught a train home, but he let Teddy come back with the hired hands as they trailed the herd north.

On the trail Teddy helped the wrangler in charge of the *remuda*—the extra horses. The following summer when his father's cattle were turned out to the range, Teddy helped the Texas farmhands tend them. By this time most of the cowboys working in Nebraska and other northern states were Texans who had trailed cattle north and then decided to stay. Teddy Abbott camped on the range with the men, cooked his grub (food) out of doors like they did, and listened to their stories.

Teddy learned to ride well, and often competed in pony races with Pawnee boys from the nearby reservation. He became an expert at cutting the particular animal he wanted from a herd. He gained experience handling steers. To break in a couple of unruly steers he fastened them both to a yoke, tied their tails together and turned them loose in a field for two or three days.

For a few weeks when he was fifteen, Teddy joined a Texas outfit trailing a herd through Nebraska. They were delivering part of the herd to a rancher and they took Teddy along because he knew the country. His first night out a violent storm set off a stampede. When morning came one man was missing. His horse had stepped into a gopher hole. Horse and rider had gone down and the stampeding cattle trampled both of them to death.

Stampedes happened frequently on the trail. The cowboy's job was to prevent stampedes and if they happened, then to control them.

When he turned eighteen Teddy Abbott left home for good. He drifted from ranch to ranch along the Platte River until he hired out with an outfit delivering a herd to the Pine Ridge Indian agency in South Dakota. At that time the federal government provided beef cattle to feed Indians on reservations. When that job was over, Teddy rode south to Austin, Texas. There he joined an outfit that was going "up the trail" to Kansas. By this time, this meant the Western Trail to Dodge City, which replaced the Chisholm Trail in the late 1870s.

By nineteen, Teddy Abbott considered himself a man, "a top cowhand, doing a top hand's work." And so he was. Like most cowboys, he had a nickname—Teddy Blue. Talking about his career years later, he said his becoming

A Cowboy Nickname

The tradition of cowboy nicknames was fairly standard. E.C."Teddy Blue" Abbott acquired his in a music hall theater in a Montana cow town. He had gone backstage, then changed his mind. As he started to turn around, his spur caught on a carpet and he fell through a thin partition onto the stage.

Years later, he explained that he thought if you were before an audience, you ought to do something. So he grabbed a chair from one of the musicians and straddled it and bucked it around the stage while he yelled, "Whoa, Blue! Whoa, Blue!" — a cowpuncher's expression at the time. When the stage manager yelled, "Hey, Blue, come out of there," the audience roared with laughter. That night when he left the theater, said Teddy, "I was Blue, and Teddy Blue I have been for fifty-five years."

a top cowhand was not so surprising. After all, that was all he'd ever thought about and he had listened to Texas cowboys and watched them and "studied the disposition of cattle" since he was ten or eleven. Besides, he said, if you started in as a kid and did only one thing all of your life you were bound to "get your head full of it," especially if you liked what you were doing.

Teddy Blue was not the only cowpuncher infected with trail fever as a kid. In Alabama during the Civil War, when Branch Isbell was eleven, Confederate soldiers herded 300 Texas steers into his mother's cornfield to pasture overnight. When they left the next morning, Branch persuaded his mom to let him ride with them as far as the Tombigbee River, four miles away.

Like cowboys everywhere, as the men moved the herd they sang over and over a song one of the men had made up. Years later, Branch remembered two of the verses—sort of a nineteenth century cowpuncher version of modern rap:

Driving cattle's our promotion
Which just exactly suits my notion,
And we perform with great devotion,
There's work enough for all.
I'd like to be a Virginia picket,
But I'd rather be in the cattle thicket
Where the hooting owl and screaming cricket
Make noise enough for all."

When Branch returned home that night, he told his mother that when he reached manhood he intended to go to Texas and be a cowpuncher. Once he turned nineteen he did just that. He took a boat to Corpus Christi, Texas, where he found a job helping to trail a herd to Abilene, Kansas.

Because he was a tenderfoot—a beginner—Branch worked as a drag rider at the back of the herd, urging on the slower animals. The herd Branch was trailing included both young steers (castrated males raised for beef) and half-grown cows (females). Quite a few calves were born along the way. Since they were not able to keep up with the herd, Branch was told to shoot them—standard practice on most long cattle drives. Branch hated the job and was so disgusted with six-shooters that from then on he never owned or used one.

Once the cattle were delivered Branch started

Young men in the West were attracted to being cowboys by the prospect of a life in the out-of-doors.

Children in the West

This editorial from the Galveston *News* of August 16, 1866, reflected how some adults felt about young people wanting to become cowpunchers:

"Our youths have souls above the mechanical arts. The little children, as early as they can walk, pilfer their mother's tape and make lassos to rope the kittens and the ducks. The boys, as soon as they can climb on a pony, are off to the prairie to drive stock. As they advance toward manhood, their highest ambition is to conquer a pitching mustang or throw a wild beef by the tail."

back to Texas, riding one horse and leading another with his gear. He got as far as Newton, 60 miles south of Abilene, and was offered a job at a camp near Cowskin Creek, watering and grazing a big herd of steers being fattened for shipment east. Branch worked at that job for a few months. Then he sold his horses and took the train to St. Louis and New Orleans, and the steamboat to Corpus Christi.

Another tenderfoot, H. D. Gruene, was nineteen when he helped trail cattle from Texas to Abilene in 1870. After the outfit spent several weeks in Abilene, a Wyoming rancher bought the herd and asked the men to trail it on to Cheyenne. Most of the cowboys quit the herd and went home, but Gruene and three others agreed to stay on. In Cheyenne, a different rancher bought the herd and asked the men to deliver it to Bear River in Utah.

Though young Gruene had started out as a tenderfoot, on the two drives he had grown wiser. He told the trail boss he would stay on only if his pay were doubled from the usual $30 a month to $60. Also he wanted a promise that he would not have to work as a drag rider at the rear of the herd. The boss agreed and Gruene completed the rest of the drive. When it was over he collected his pay in $20 gold pieces. He had what he called a "general cleaning up," bought new clothes, and headed for Texas—taking the train as far as Abilene and continuing from there on horseback.

Thunderstorms on the trail were common, but cowboys always dreaded them. The first crack of thunder could start a stampede, and lightning was a major cause of death for both men and animals on the trail. On Perry Robuck's first cattle drive, at sixteen, he marveled at the eerie phenomenon called St. Elmo's fire, or fox fire, a common sight for seasoned cowboys. Rather than streaks of lightning, the dull phosphorescent light of fox fire might roll along the ground in a ball, or play on the cattle's horns and on the ears of the horses. Occasionally there was the scary sight of fire snaking over the backs of the cattle and along the horses' manes.

Life on the trail included such necessary hardships as spending many nights sleeping out in the open no matter what the weather was.

On that drive, young Robuck often slept on rain-soaked blankets and had to wear wet clothing for several days and nights at a time. Even so, a chance to rope buffalo and see sights he had never seen before made up for the unpleasant parts of the drive.

Many cowboys in the late 1800s had worked around cattle as kids. They had helped a relative with ranch jobs or rounded up milk cows for a neighbor. When J. C. Thompson went on his first drive at seventeen, he did not consider himself a novice in the business. For he had already had years of experience gathering, roping, and branding mavericks (unbranded or orphaned animals.)

When Texas cowboy Billie Krempkau was young, he went onto the open range and brought in cows with young calves to sell to local dairymen. At fifteen, he left school to help a neighbor who broke wild mules—that is, taught them to be more gentle and to work so they could be sold to the government as pack animals. Young Krempkau learned to rope a wild mule, then tie bags of sand on the animal's back and lead it around until it got used to carrying a load. The mule bucked and jumped at first, but by the third day it usually calmed down.

Billie Krempkau then worked for a couple of years as a freighter—a driver in charge of a train of mules hauling trade goods to Mexico. By the time he turned seventeen he knew enough about riding and roping to get a trail job, and soon after, was hired to help move a herd up the Western Trail to Dodge City, Kansas.

Cattle were not the only animals James Walker learned to handle as a kid. At fifteen, Walker's first ranch job—for $7 a month—was herding cattle on a ranch north of San Antonio. He quit to join the Confederate Army, and tried to enlist at the nearby camp, where his two brothers were

Maverick, Cowpuncher, and Dogie

The word "maverick" comes from Samuel A. Maverick, a Texas lawyer. By the 1860s it meant an unbranded or orphaned animal. A popular theory as to how the word first acquired that meaning is this: Sam Maverick received about 400 cattle as payment for a debt. The man he hired to look after the herd, was so careless about branding or earmarking new calves that soon strays were wandering all over the range. Around 1855, Maverick sold his land, cattle, and brand. When the new owner hired men to hunt down the unmarked animals for Maverick, the over-eager searchers branded and claimed as "Maverick's" every stray that they found.

Soon, any orphaned or unmarked animal was called a "maverick." "To maverick" meant to mark and brand any stray. There were so many unbranded strays around after the Civil War that mavericking was common. Today the word maverick has come to mean one who is independent and unattached to a cause—especially a political party.

The term "cowpuncher," for cowboy, comes from the 1880s when many cattle were shipped by train. Cowboys used prod poles to urge the animals into the railroad cars, and to "punch up" or get back on their feet any cattle that had lain down.

A "dogie" was an orphan calf whose mother was dead or missing. Later, dogies came to mean any animals—even a whole herd—that cowboys felt friendly toward.

Cutting out a calf ("dogie") from the herd, probably to be left on the range until next year.

stationed. At first the commanding officer turned him down because he was too young, but then relented and let Walker sign up. When most of the men at the camp were transferred to South Texas, James Walker and a few other young recruits were left to guard the post. By then the horses were gone, but Walker was assigned to tend the camp's 75 camels, used as army pack animals. They gave him no end of trouble. All winter the camels refused to eat grass. To keep them from starving young Walker had to send to San Antonio for corn to feed the stubborn creatures. When the war ended, Walker, still in his teens, was glad to go back to herding cattle again.

TWO

Shawnee Trail

By the time Texas became a state in 1845, Texas herders were driving small numbers of cattle north to St. Louis along an old Indian trading path they called simply "the trail." Texas-bound settlers who followed that same route called it the Texas Road. Herders driving cattle north in the 1850s knew it as the Kansas Trail. No one is sure exactly when it acquired the name Shawnee Trail.

The trail began just south of San Antonio, in the heart of Texas cattle raising country. It curved northeast along what was then the Texas frontier, passing through the tiny settlement of Dallas, and continuing north to the Red River, the northern border of Texas. Federal surveyors in 1841 had laid out this Texas portion of the trail as a military road. To protect Texas settlers against Native American raids, the government built forts along the road.

The best spot to ford the Red River was at Rock Bluff Crossing, where the sloping riverbanks made it easier for cattle to get in and out of the water. The cows had to swim across, but a log raft ferried the wagons. Beyond the Red River, the trail passed through Indian Territory (now the state of Oklahoma), home of what were called the Five Civilized Tribes. These Cherokees, Creeks, Seminoles, Chickasaws, and Choctaws had been moved west in the early 1800s from parts of Tennessee, North Carolina, Georgia, Alabama, Arkansas, and Mississippi to make room for non-Indian settlers in those states.

Throughout Indian Territory bands of warriors often stopped the drovers (cattle drivers) to demand payment for crossing their lands. Toll was usually one beef (steer)—or in some cases, a beef for each day the drovers were on an Indian group's land. If a trail boss refused to pay up, the Indians waved blankets or yelled to start a stampede—and got their beefs that way.

In the land of the Choctaw, the trail later known as Shawnee came to Boggy Depot on Clear Boggy Creek. The creek lived up to its name. On drives north, cattle often got stuck in the wet, soggy marsh. Sometimes cowboys and their horses spent an exhausting day or more trying to pull the animals out.

About 65 miles from Boggy Depot, the trail crossed into Creek country and then into the land of the Cherokee. Soon after, it reached Fort Gibson. The fort was one of a string of military stockades the U.S. government built in the early 1800s to keep peace along the frontier in Indian Territory, Kansas, and western Arkansas. Beyond Fort Gibson, the trail followed the Osage Trace, an ancient Indian trading path used by the Osage people. It led from Baxter Springs in the southeastern corner of Kansas to St. Louis, Missouri.

At times, traffic on the Shawnee Trail was heavy. Herds of bawling Texas longhorns going north shared the wide and dusty path with southbound settlers' Conestoga wagons, military caravans, and mule-drawn freight wagons headed for Santa Fe.

By 1854 so many outlaws in southwestern Missouri were attacking cowmen and stealing their livestock that

From Texas to New York

Although the railhead at St. Louis was the final goal for most Texas cattle drives in the 1850s, in 1852 an Illinois cowman named Tom Candy Ponting had more ambitious plans. He intended to trail cattle from Texas all the way to Illinois, and possibly farther. Late in that year Ponting and

Cattle being driven through the streets of New York City after arrival from the West sometimes caused confusion and injuries.

his partner, Washington Malone—their buckskin belts weighted down with gold coins—rode west to buy Texas cattle. They gathered 600 head from several different ranches in northeastern Texas. In Indian Territory they bought 80 more cattle—hefty steers, each weighing close to 1,200 pounds. Then the Illinois cowmen started home.

To keep their herd from straying, the men hung a bell around the neck of an ox and tied the animal to the back of their wagon. The steers obediently followed the belled ox. At St. Louis, men and animals crossed the Mississippi River by ferry, where the main task was to keep the cattle from jumping into the river.

Ponting and Malone arrived back in central Illinois on July 26, 1853—around nine months after their journey began. They gave the animals a long rest, and the following spring trailed the best 150 of them east to Muncie, Indiana. There, they loaded the cattle onto railroad cars bound for New York City. They unloaded the animals at several stops along the way for exercise. From Bergen Hill, New Jersey, they trailed their cattle to the Hudson River ferry. Once across the Hudson they drove the herd through the streets of New York to the Hundred Street Market. There Ponting sold the steers after one of the longest trail drives ever—1,500 miles "on the hoof" and 600 miles by rail car.

some Texas cattle herders stopped taking their animals to St. Louis. Instead, from Baxter Springs they followed an old military road along the Kansas border until they reached the Missouri River. There they crossed over into Missouri to sell their cattle in the western Missouri towns of Kansas City, Independence, or Westport. Here they found buyers eager for Texas cattle. Butchers, Indian agents, and army supply officers needed Texas beef. So did midwestern feeders—persons who bought the animals to

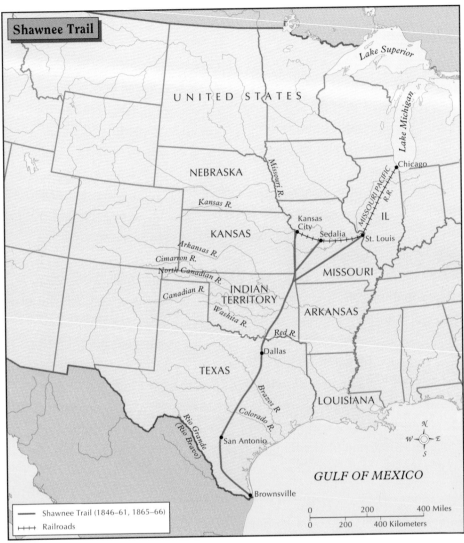

The earliest cattle trail, the Shawnee Trail established prior to the Civil War, began in southern Texas and ended at the railheads in Missouri.

fatten up in their stockyards for later sale. Westbound emigrants wanted the Texas cattle to start herds when they finally reached their new homesteads in Utah or Oregon.

Despite the ready market for Texas cattle, in the early 1850s domestic cattle along the Shawnee Trail began to

Cattle for California

Mormon emigrants brought cattle when they came West to settle in Utah Territory, and their leader, Brigham Young, encouraged the Mormons to use part of their herds to pay tithes (part of their yearly income) to the Church. Soon the Church had many cattle on its grazing grounds on Antelope Island in the Great Salt Lake. After the Gold Rush of 1849, Mormon volunteers trailed the Church's herds to California where wealthy miners were willing to pay for the cattle with gold.

Utah cattlemen also built up herds by trading with westbound emigrants on the trail to Oregon, whose animals had traveled long distances. Trading one good cow for two or three worn-out cows—which they cared for and fed until the animals were again in good shape—these Utah cattle owners then drove the healthy cattle to markets on the West coast.

The Utah drovers went to northern California by way of the Great Salt Lake and present-day Winemucca, Nevada. To reach southern California, they joined an old Spanish trail that ran from Santa Fe through southwest Utah to Los Angeles.

Some Texans drove cattle west along a southern trail through Arizona. Other Texans trailed their herds north to Utah by way of Colorado and then wintered the herds at Browns Hole in the northeast corner of Utah. In the spring they moved north into Idaho and then continued west to California. Although the Texans were on the trail most of the year, the high prices for beef in California made the journey worth it.

After the late 1850s, the market for cattle in California waned as Californians developed large herds of their own and no longer needed to import their beef.

suffer or die from a disease that people called "Texas fever." At the time, no one knew what caused the disease since the long-horned Texas cattle seemed to be immune, but the domestic cattle they passed along the way were not. Much later it was found that ticks on the Texas cattle were the cause.

Missouri farmers blamed the Texas longhorns for bringing the disease north, and they objected to having the animals trailed past their farms. Some angry farmers threatened to kill any Texas cattle that entered their counties. In 1855, Missouri lawmakers passed a quarantine bill that prohibited anyone from trailing diseased animals into or through the state and a few years later the Kansas legislature passed a bill prohibiting *all* Texas cattle. Despite the laws and the farmers' threats, a few Texans still trailed their herds north over the Shawnee Trail.

The start of the Civil War in 1860 brought an abrupt end to Texas cattle trailing. With no army during the war to protect them from Native Americans, many Texans living on the frontier deserted their ranches and left the stock to run wild. Those still trying to operate their ranches were so shorthanded that they could not brand all of the cattle, and many animals strayed. When the Civil War ended in 1865, those Texans who had left home came back to find thousands of unbranded cattle roaming the plains.

At the same time, Texans heard about a new stockyard in Chicago where packers—eager for beef to feed meat-deprived easterners once the war was over—were paying $40 a head for Texas cattle worth only $5 at home. With that good news, many Texans built up herds by hunting and branding the strays they called mavericks.

By March 1866, more than a quarter of a million cattle were ready to go north on the Shawnee Trail. Returning

African-American and Hispanic Cowboys

During the heyday of cattle trailing, from 1865 to 1890, more than 35,000 cowboys rode the trails. About 5,000 of them were Mexican and 5,000 were African American—mostly ex-slaves who had worked on Texas ranches. African-American cowboy Henry Beckwith was known as "the Coyote" for his ability to hunt at night the wild Texas longhorns hiding in the thick bush. Nat Love, son of Tennessee slaves, left home at fifteen to work as a cowboy in Texas. After a few years Love became a rodeo star, and in 1907 wrote a book about his adventures.

When their cowpunching days were over, many other African-American and Mexican cowboys joined rodeos as trick riders, ropers, and bronco busters. One of the most famous was Bill Pickett who added the word "bull-dogging" to the cowboy's language for his unique way of bringing down a steer without using a lasso. Pickett would grab and twist the steer's head, then—like a bulldog—clamp onto its upper lip with his teeth. With the Miller Brothers traveling rodeo Bill Pickett joined Will Rogers, a roper who later became a famous humorist, and Tom Mix, a trick rider who became a cowboy movie star.

Typical African-American cowboys included Nat Love (above) and the two men (left).

soldiers, former slaves, and anyone else in need of a job could easily find work helping to drive cattle north. The herders would get their pay when the animals were sold at trail's end. Since the closest railhead for Texas was Sedalia, Missouri, that's where many of the cattle were driven.

Farmers were still worried about the spread of Texas fever, however. At the borders of Kansas and Missouri, volunteer guards tried to turn the Texans back. Some irate settlers and ruffians attacked the Texans and beat them. They killed some of the cowboys and sold their stock on the black market. Few cattle made it all the way to Sedalia.

Fortunately for the Texans, in 1867 a midwestern cattle buyer named Joseph G. McCoy arrived in Kansas to solve their problem. McCoy urged Texas herders to forget the Shawnee Trail and Sedalia, and instead, to bring their herds north over a new trail to a railway point in central Kansas. From there they could ship their cattle east by train and avoid trouble with disgruntled farmers and angry mobs along the Kansas-Missouri border.

Since the new railroad now reached as far west as Abilene, Kansas, that was where McCoy decided to build a large number of cattle pens. He would then invite Texas cattlemen to bring their herds north to Abilene.

THREE

"String 'Em Out..."

The first step for a long cattle drive was to collect the animals to be trailed. In Texas in the early 1800s the long-horned cattle were as wild as deer and just as hard to hunt. After a few years, however, the longhorns had mixed with other cattle and grew used to seeing cowboys on horseback and so were easily rounded up.

To get an early start while there was plenty of grass, Texas ranchers trailing their herds north held their roundups in the spring. About 20 cowhands took part, with a range or roundup boss in charge. The cook brought his chuck wagon to the camp, and the horse wrangler was in charge of the remuda. Before sunrise on the first day of the roundup the range boss sent the cowhands out to search for cattle. All day the men flushed cattle out of brush thickets and canyons and herded them back to the camp.

The next day the cowboys "cut out" the cattle to be left on the range—usually calves and their mothers. Certain horses were especially good at "cutting out." They knew when to turn sharply and stop, to frighten an animal from the herd and keep it out. The easiest way to get a calf was to bring out its mother and the calf would follow.

Once a cow was cut from the herd a cowboy used his lariat to rope it by the head or feet. A good roping horse

Branding and Earmarking

The brand on a steer or cow's side and the mark on the ear were the only ways to identify a rancher's animal. To keep rustlers from altering the brand on animals they had stolen, the ranchers preferred brands that were hard to change. Each ranch's brand and earmark were recorded in brand books in various states. The brand might be initials, symbols, words, or pictographs (pictures representing words)—such as Lazy Z, Tumbling R, Scissors, Frying Pan, Double Circle, etc. The earmark was a nick at the upper or lower edge of the ear, a triangle nipped from the tip, or a square cut across the bottom of the ear. If the flappy part of the ear was deeply split it was called the jingle bob.

Two hundred years earlier, the Spanish conqueror Cortes began the practice of branding cattle in Mexico by marking three crosses on the side of each of his animals, between ribs and hip. The first Texas brands were usually the owner's initials.

B Browning Brothers	**M** Rocking M, Mcpherson Cattle Co.	**WF** Wells Fargo
Z Meathook Cattle Co.	**Mc** Running Mᶜ, McInture Ranch	**X** Bar X Bar, Scorup Somerville Cattle Co.

A few examples of brands used by ranchers.

would stop the instant the lariat was snubbed tight around the saddle horn and the roped animal fell. Then the cow or calf was dragged or herded to the bonfire where the branding iron was heating. As soon as the cowboys had pressed the hot iron against the animal's side they turned it loose. If a rancher was putting together a herd with cattle from different ranches, all of the animals to be trailed were pushed single file through a narrow branding chute and "road branded" with a second brand.

Next, the cowboys caught and branded horses for the remuda. They chose from the many small horses that ran wild in Texas, descendants of early Spanish horses. These tough and wiry animals had to be broken, or "busted"— trained to be ridden with saddle and bridle. This took about a week. Often a rancher hired a "buster"—an expert who went from ranch to ranch plying his special trade. A long cattle drive required a remuda of from six to ten mounts for each cowboy. A hard working horse had to rest after a few hours, so a cowboy changed mounts at least twice a day. Also the cowboys needed horses better able to do certain jobs. Some horses were used for trail riding, others for roping. Good cutting horses had to be able to turn quickly and stop suddenly. Horses used for night herding had to be gentle and sure footed. They needed keen eyesight and a sense of direction, for if a cowboy dozed in the saddle during his two-hour watch it was up to the horse to head off an escaping animal.

When the remuda was ready and the herd organized, the drive could begin. The wrangler's job was to trail the remuda by day, and make sure the horses did not stray at

Horses were rounded up, here in a rope corral, and then selected for the drive.

night. For leading the herd, the trail boss picked out one or two big, strong steers. He chose animals that seemed naturally to take their places at the front and stay there, while other cattle were content to follow. Around their necks the lead animals wore bells that jingled as they walked. Work oxen often made good leaders since they were seldom afraid to cross streams.

On a long drive, one cowboy could handle between 200 and 300 cattle, so for a herd of 2,500 head the trail boss needed a dozen cowboys. The most experienced were the point riders, who rode beside the lead steers to keep them heading in the proper direction. To turn the herd to the right, the right point man dropped back and the point man on the left rode ahead and started pushing the cattle over.

Swing riders rode farther back, where the herd began to spread wider. Still farther back, on either side, were the flank riders. At the rear, breathing all the trail dust, were the drag riders, the green (inexperienced) hands whose job was to prod the drags—cattle too lame or weak to keep up.

Lead Steers

Although most lead steers were sold with the rest of the herd once the outfit reached the railroad, favorite lead steers were often kept to lead new herds the following season. Cattleman Charles Goodnight used the steer he named Old Blue to lead herds for seven years. During those years, Old Blue—wearing a brass bell around his neck—led 10,000 head of cattle on long drives. The huge 1,400 pound steer came to be like a pet and wandered freely around the camp mooching handouts from the cowboys. Old Blue was finally retired to pasture, to live out his old age in peace.

Sometimes, driving the cattle was uneventful enough for a friendly conversation.

Even with bandannas tied over their faces the drag riders could collect dust half an inch deep on their hats and eyebrows. Some cowboys refused to work with the drags. They would rather ask for their time—collect their pay—and quit the herd.

The horse wrangler and remuda usually set out ahead with the cook and with the trail boss who scouted for water and good camping places. The wrangler was often the youngest hand, perhaps a kid who wanted to become a cowboy, or the herd owner's son. When the older men had time, they gave him tips on riding and roping.

A good trail boss did more than merely walk his herd to market. The purpose of the drive for Texans was to arrive at the shipping point with animals that were fat and in good shape when they were finally sold. At the start of the long drive, the trail boss let the herd graze along the way to get the animals used to the routine. The idea was to ease them gradually in the right direction without letting them know they were being pushed. At watering spots, the trail

The trail boss managed to view the herd from a vantage point on higher ground.

boss made sure to spread the cattle along the bank with the lead cattle headed downstream. That way they drank clear water, and as the slower drags arrived they were farther upstream so they drank clear water, too. If the animals were tired or losing too much weight, the trail boss might stay in one place for a day or two to let them rest and graze.

An outfit trailing a herd north could cover from 10 to 15 miles a day, barring emergencies such as flooded rivers or rustlers. Usually cattle crossed rivers by fording (wading across) or swimming. Most steers swam well and seemed to enjoy it. Rustlers were more troublesome. It was easy for these cattle thieves to stampede a herd and make off with several animals. Then with a heated metal rod they altered the brand—for example turning 1 into 7, C into O, S into 8, or P into B.

Each day around 12 o'clock, the outfit "nooned"— stopped for the midday meal that cowboys called dinner. If the cook had enough headstart, he cooked a hot meal. Otherwise, he served leftovers from breakfast. While the cattle rested or grazed, the men ate in shifts, with two riders always circling the herd to make sure that no animals strayed. After an hour the trail boss got on his horse and waved his hat, the signal that it was time to "string 'em out" and begin the drive again.

Although the cattle had mingled when watering and grazing, when they were back on the trail they found their same places. The lead steers were back in the lead. The cattle who had been in the middle stayed in the middle. The drags remained the drags.

In late afternoon on the trail, the outfit camped for the night. The trail boss tried to pick a spot off the trail with fresh grass for the cattle to eat, dry grass for them to lie on, and no deep ravines into which they might plunge in a stampede. Supper was much like dinner and breakfast— black coffee, sourdough biscuits, meat and gravy, beans, canned or dried fruit. Once in a great while the cook found time to bake an apple or raisin pie.

Around dusk the men bedded the herd. The cowboys circled the cattle, riding around and around to drive the herd into as small a space as possible. Their hope was to keep the herd that way. Through the night the men worked in pairs, each pair guarding the bedded herd for two hours. Since the cowboys did not wear wristwatches they judged when their time was up by the position of the North Star. Often a horse had a better sense of time than its rider. After two hours it would start edging toward camp.

As the cowboys circled in opposite directions around the

Crossing a river was often a dangerous adventure on the trail.

Cowboy Songs

Whether they had good voices or not, cowboys sang a lot—not only to calm nervous herds while on the trail, but also when the cattle were penned up in a cow town ready to be loaded onto a railroad car. It was said that a trail boss didn't like to hire a cowboy who couldn't sing.

Sometimes cowboys sang sentimental ballads they had learned back home. If a certain song seemed to quiet a herd during a thunderstorm, they'd sing that same song every time it stormed. They sang church hymns, lullabies, and doleful songs about lonesome cowpunchers, midnight stampedes, bucking horses, and sudden death. As Teddy Blue Abbott once observed, "Cowboys loved to sing about people dying...I guess it was because they was so full of life themselves."

One especially clear night when Teddy Blue and his partner were on guard and the cattle were quiet, the two men took turns singing verses of a song. One would sing a verse, then from across the herd the partner would answer with another verse. They kept this up for the whole two-hour shift.

sleeping cattle they crooned slow-moving hymns or ballads—the sadder the better—to soothe the animals and keep them calm. A cowboy's greatest dread was for a startled or frightened herd to stampede. Almost anything could spook (scare) a nervous herd. Thunder and lightning, certainly, but even the snap of a twig or someone sneezing could set the animals off. It was a rare drive that did not have at least one or two stampedes.

In some outfits, the cowboys drew straws to see who went on night watch first. The rest sat around the campfire for a while telling stories or singing. They went to bed early, to get rested before their turn to guard the herd.

A guitar was too big and bulky to take on a cattle drive, but many cowboys had harmonicas. A few brought their fiddles. One cowboy fiddler had other cowboys on horseback lead his horse as he circled a herd so his hands were free to play his instrument.

Cowboys sang at other times, too. They chose the song depending on where they were, and they let the pony's gait set the rhythm of the song. If the cowboys were at the back, riding drag and trying to get the slow ones to speed up, they sang songs that were loud and vigorous. For day riding, there were lively songs such as "Git Along Little Dogies, Git Along." If cowboys were riding trotting horses they sang songs with lots of verses that went on and on. A classic among cowboy songs, because so many cowboys used the trail, was *The Old Chisholm Trail*. The first of its many verses began:

"Come along, boys, and listen to my tale;
I'll tell you my troubles on the old Chisholm Trail.
Come a ti yi yippy, yippy yay, yippy yay
Come a ti yi yippy, yippy yay."

Before wrapping himself in his blanket the cowboy tethered his horse close by. Some men slept with the reins in their hands, in order to be up and in their saddles as quickly as possible in case of a stampede.

Before the cook went to bed he studied the sky to locate the North Star. Then he turned the wagon tongue, pointing it north. For Texans heading for Kansas, this was important. If the morning was overcast they would still know in which direction to go. The cook was always last to turn in and the first one up each morning. Before sunrise he was out of his bedroll to build up the fire so he could start making breakfast. Then, with a loud call to "Arise and shine!"

Cowboy Clothes

The clothes cowboys wore were fairly standard. That was because every item of clothing was useful, and had a reason for being the way it was.

The cowboy's hat was the last thing he took off when he went to bed, and the first thing he put on in the morning. It was usually made of felt (compacted wool) and was sturdy enough for hard use. Its wide brim shaded the cowboy's eyes from the burning sun and protected his head from rain or hailstones. Most cowboy hats were dove-gray or light brown. Many men decorated their hats with a band—perhaps a woven horsehair band, a string of Indian beads, or a rattlesnake skin.

The cowboy's hat was useful. With it he could fan a campfire into life, or carry water to put the fire out. Cowboys sometimes used their hats to beat out grass fires. Trail bosses waved their hats to signal to their men from a distance away. A cowboy could pull down his hat's wide brim to protect his ears from frostbite.

The cowboy's neckerchief had practical uses, too. The cowboy could tie down his hat in a wind with it. Knotted in back and pulled over his mouth and nose, a neckerchief kept out the dust if a cowboy was at the back of the herd riding drag. It served as a towel after he washed his face in the morning. He could blindfold a skittery horse with his neckerchief, or create a bandage, a sling for a broken arm, or a tourniquet for a snakebite.

A cowboy generally wore wool pants, a buttoned shirt of cotton or flannel, and over the shirt a vest with a deep pocket. That was where cowboys kept their pouch of Bull Durham tobacco and a tally book where they kept records of cattle numbers, brands, etc. When riding in thorny brush a cowboy wore chaps (leather leggings that fastened with a belt around the waist). A cowboy took pride in a fine pair of boots, and was willing to pay a great deal of money for boots that were custom-made. The high tops kept out gravel and twigs that the horse kicked up. The high heels on the boots prevented the rider's foot from slipping through the stirrup. The slope of the heel kept the rider from being "hung up"—hanging by one foot from the stirrup and getting dragged by the horse. When a cowboy was on foot and roping, the high heels dug into the ground and gave him a more secure footing. The spurs that fastened onto the back of the boots were also a necessary part of a cowboy's equipment. He used the spurs to nudge the horse into quick action, though all a well-trained horse usually needed was a mere touch.

Cowboys who trailed the cattle north usually owned their saddles, but not their horses. They depended on getting their mounts from the remuda (the herd of extra horses). A cowboy's 40-pound saddle was his "office." He spent most of the day in the saddle, and everything he needed for the trail was there. His lariat hung on the saddle, and when the cowboy was roping he could secure the lariat to the saddle horn. Hanging from the saddle were leather strings, or ties, for holding things like his slicker. When cowboys spoke of someone "selling his saddle" it meant he was finished in the profession. If he "sacked his saddle," it meant he had died.

A young cowboy on horseback dressed in typical attire on the trail— chaps, boots, wide-brimmed hat, saddle, and rope ready for use.

he woke up the sleeping cowboys. While the men downed a quick breakfast, the wrangler brought in the remuda so they could choose their mounts for the morning.

At the end of the long drive the men usually pastured the herd somewhere outside town. A few men stayed behind to watch over the herd while the rest collected their pay and rode into town, ready to kick up their heels and have some fun.

Some Kansas cow towns required visiting cowboys to check their "artillery" (six-shooters), along with their horses, at the local livery stable—a law not always rigidly enforced. Real cowboys were not as trigger-happy as those often shown in the movies or on television. Although the men sometimes fired a few shots in the air to let off steam when they arrived in town, what most wanted when they first arrived was a bath and a haircut. Those with moustaches got them trimmed, and maybe dyed or waxed.

The cowboy's next stop in town was the dry goods store for new clothes. A good broad-brimmed hat or a fine pair of boots could cost almost one month's pay. Local saloons, gambling tables, and dance hall girls were happy to make

At the end of a drive, one of the cowboy's next stops was to replace worn equipment, such as clothes and boots.

off with what was left. Some cowboys were broke by the time they rode back to camp to give the others in the outfit a chance to go into town.

While their grazing herds were pastured outside town getting fat on the juicy Kansas grasses, the herds' owners were in town making deals with buyers. During the early "boom" years, an owner could sell his animals in Kansas for ten times their value in Texas. Buyers were representatives from eastern slaughterhouses, army supply officers, or agents collecting food for reservations.

If the buyer was a rancher who wanted the cattle as stock animals for breeding purposes, he would have the animals re-branded, this time with his brand. Often a new owner hired the same cowboys who trailed the herd up from Texas to deliver the cattle to their next destination—perhaps to a ranch in Colorado, Utah, or Wyoming.

FOUR

Chisholm Trail

When Joseph McCoy came to Kansas in 1867, his dream was to turn Abilene into a lively shipping center for Texas cattle. At that time, Abilene, for six years a station for the Overland Stage (a stagecoach company), was little more than a few cabins with sodsoil and grass· roofs. Its half-dozen businesses included a blacksmith shop, a dry goods store, a six-room hotel, and a log-cabin saloon. Still, Joe McCoy was not concerned. For Abilene had the one feature he needed: Tracks for the still unfinished Union Pacific Railroad now reached Abilene. From Abilene, McCoy could ship Texas cattle by train to feeders and slaughterhouses in Kansas City, St. Louis, and Chicago.

In July, McCoy prepared for the Texas drovers. He began building a livery stable, a barn, a three-story hotel that could accommodate 80 guests, and a shipping yard big enough to hold a thousand cattle. Two months later, the structures were done and McCoy had checked out the most direct route for Texans to follow to Kansas. He was ready to bring in the cattle.

First, however, he told the governor of Kansas about his project. Although Kansas farmers feared that the cattle would infect their domestic herds with Texas fever, the governor approved of McCoy's plans. "I regard the opening of that cattle trail into and across western Kansas," said the governor, "of as much value to the state as is the Missouri River."

A delighted McCoy sent a friend on horseback to ride south and invite any Texas trail drivers on their way north with cattle for sale to come to Abilene. McCoy assured Texans that his new route was more direct, and had more prairie and less timberland than the old Shawnee Trail. He promised it would have "better grass and fewer flies [and] no wild Indian disturbances."

The trail that McCoy urged Texans to follow to Abilene came to be known as the Chisholm Trail. It was named for Indian trader Jesse Chisholm, son of a Scottish father and a Cherokee mother. Chisholm spoke a dozen Native American languages and had worked as a translator and guide in Indian Territory and knew it well. He had established trading posts there, and had also brought trade goods from Kansas trading posts to exchange for the Indians' furs, buffalo robes, or cattle. On one of his trading excursions, a year before the Civil War ended, Jesse Chisholm blazed a trail that was straight and level enough for his wagon to follow easily. From then on, Chisholm used that wagon route regularly. So did other white and Indian traders and travelers, who often called it "Chisholm's Trail."

The first Texas cowmen to bring herds to Abilene followed the trail Chisholm had blazed. Although his

Half-Cherokee and half-Scottish, Jesse Chisholm blazed a new trail to get supplies for his trading posts in Indian Territory.

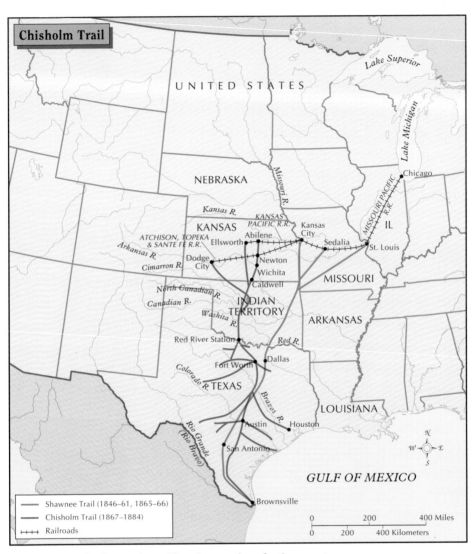

Chisholm Trail

UNITED STATES

Lake Superior

Lake Michigan

NEBRASKA

Missouri R.

Chicago

Kansas R.

KANSAS
PACIFIC R.R.

KANSAS

Kansas
City

IL

ATCHISON, TOPEKA
& SANTE FE R.R.
Arkansas R.

Ellsworth

Abilene

Sedalia

MISSOURI PACIFIC R.R.

St. Louis

Dodge
City

Newton

Cimarron R.

Wichita

Caldwell

MISSOURI

North Canadian R.

INDIAN
TERRITORY

Canadian R.

ARKANSAS

Washita R.

Red River Station

Red R.

Colorado R.

Fort Worth

Dallas

TEXAS

Brazos R.

LOUISIANA

Austin

Houston

Rio Grande
(Rio Bravo)

San Antonio

N
W — E
S

GULF OF MEXICO

Brownsville

— Shawnee Trail (1846–61, 1865–66)
— Chisholm Trail (1867–1884)
+++ Railroads

0   200   400 Miles
0   200   400 Kilometers

The Chisholm Trail met the railheads at points farther west
in Kansas than the Shawnee Trail.

route only covered parts of Indian Territory and Kansas,
most people later gave the name Chisholm Trail to the
entire trail from Brownsville, in the southernmost tip of
Texas, to Abilene, Kansas.

The first year that McCoy's Abilene stock pens opened

Texans brought 35,000 head of cattle north, enough to fill 20 railroad cars bound for the East. Pleased with his success, McCoy wrote letters to Texas cattle ranchers and newspapers describing his new trail. To attract buyers, he placed advertisements in Missouri and Illinois newspapers. And to stay on the good side of Abilene residents, McCoy paid money to any settlers whose fields had been trampled by Texas longhorns.

To make the journey north easier for Texans, McCoy hired surveyors to straighten and shorten parts of the route. Since his trail was less traveled and less well marked than the old Shawnee Trail, he had workers pile mounds of dirt as markers to guide the herders to Abilene.

The following summer, many herds arrived from Texas and more than a thousand carloads of cattle were shipped to the East. Then—with cattle still waiting in Abilene— McCoy suddenly ran out of buyers. The main reason was

Cattle drovers herding Texas longhorns into a railroad car at Abilene, Kansas, along the Kansas-Pacific Railway.

not concern about Texas fever, but the fact that not all midwestern buyers knew that Abilene had cattle for sale.

To publicize the town, McCoy put together a "wild west circus." He hired several Texas cowboys and Mexican ropers from California to capture wild horses, elk, and buffalo—including a giant buffalo bull that weighed over a ton. The animals were loaded into stock cars that had been reinforced. Wide and gaudy canvas banners hanging on the outside of the cars advertised the cattle bargains to be found in Abilene. The troupe traveled to St. Louis and Chicago where the animals were displayed and the men performed before large crowds. The Texans with their colorful bandannas, boots, and spurs and the Mexicans with their bright shirts and red sashes were a big hit. The men did roping and riding stunts and threw wild steers with and without a lariat. The audiences loved it. Besides staging this wild west show, McCoy brought several Illinois cattlemen to Kansas for a free buffalo hunt. These two public relations stunts helped McCoy achieve his purpose: to put Abilene on the map at last. Eastern feeders flocked to the small Kansas cow town to buy Texas cattle and Abilene's cattle market boomed.

By 1868 enough hoofprints led from Texas to Abilene so that the entire Chisholm Trail was well marked. The basic trail had dozens of branches as cowboys from all parts of Texas gathered cattle together to trail north.

In southern Texas the Chisholm and old Shawnee Trails followed the same route. From the Rio Grande both trails led to San Antonio. Like most cattle towns along the way, San Antonio had plenty of gambling halls and saloons as well as places to buy provisions.

Beyond San Antonio were grasslands for grazing as drovers moved their herds north. At Austin, north of San

Antonio, cowmen found easy crossings along the Colorado River. Getting their herds over the Brazos River at Waco was harder. After a rain the Brazos could be treacherous, often impossible to cross for days. After 1870 the new toll bridge at Waco made the crossing easier, but the drovers had to pay five cents an animal, so most still took their chances and swam their herds across.

North of the village of Waco, the Chisholm and Shawnee Trails split. Drovers following the Shawnee went north to Dallas, but by the late 1860s most Texans veered northwest on the Chisholm Trail to the frontier town of Fort Worth. Here the cook and the trail boss had their last chance to stock up on food and supplies, such as extra saddles or rope, before heading through Indian Territory. Instead of going on, some drovers sold their herds here and returned home.

A reconstructed general store along the trail, stocked with provisions.

The journey from Fort Worth to the Red River crossing at Red River Station took about a week. The Red River was one of the most dangerous on the Chisholm Trail. Besides the quicksands in some places, the river could flood after a storm even as a herd was crossing. More cowboys drowned in the Red than in any other river on the trail.

Once over the river, the Chisholm Trail pointed straight north through Indian Territory. About 30 miles in—a two-day journey—drovers came to Stinking Creek, a favorite campground. On a high flat plateau above the creek lay a jumble of reddish sandstone boulders and flat rocks. Early herders stacked some of the rocks into two enormous piles, 10 feet high and 300 feet apart. These trail markers could be seen from either direction by drovers 10 or 15 miles away. Many cowboys passing by carved initials or brands on the soft rocks with knives or spurs. They called the plateau Monument Hill.

Farther north was Washita Creek, which was sometimes flooded, and horses and cattle had to swim across. The men made log rafts to get the wagons to the other side. The Cimarron was another river that could cause trouble. Herders tried to drive their cattle across quickly before any animals stopped to drink and got bogged down in the Cimarron's quicksands.

In the northern part of Indian Territory, drovers often had to wait while vast herds of buffalo crossed the trail. The men had to take care that none of their cattle—or even the horses—joined the buffalo herds. The drive through Indian Territory on the Chisholm Trail took about a month. As drovers crossed into Kansas they passed what would soon become the border town of Caldwell. Beyond here,

Cattle train leaving Ellsworth, Kansas, for Kansas City and points east.

the trail to Abilene led across prairie land dotted with patches of goldenrod and sunflowers.

For five years, Abilene was the reigning cow town in Kansas. Every summer and fall, thousands of cattle arrived. Most were shipped East, but some were bought by Nebraska ranchers who had them trailed farther north. At first, the merchants and townspeople of Abilene welcomed the extra business the drovers brought. Soon, though, the residents grew tired of rowdy cowboys swarming into

Wild Bill Hickok

For a time, Abilene's marshal was James Butler (Wild Bill) Hickok, ex-teamster, stagecoach driver, federal scout, and guerrilla fighter—and the best known gunman of the old West. Besides bringing law and order to Abilene, Wild Bill liked to show off his skill as an expert marksman: throwing a coin in the air and hitting it with a bullet before it reached the ground, tossing up a hat and riddling its brim with bullet holes as it spun in the air, or keeping a tomato can dancing in the dust.

As a scout, Wild Bill had worn buckskins. Later he switched to fancier clothes—often checkered pants, a long "Prince Albert" coat, cowboy boots with patent leather tops, and an embroidered silk vest. Some time after working as a lawman, Wild Bill Hickok joined Buffalo Bill's Wild West Show for a season.

James "Wild Bill" Hickok

town every summer. And they objected to the many saloons, gambling houses, and dance halls that crowded the main street, attracting not only boisterous cowhands but also cheating gamblers and trigger-happy outlaws.

Settlers outside town resented cattle herds trampling their cornfields and muddying their water holes. Many demanded money from the drovers for damage done. Some threatened to sue. Finally in 1872 a group of farmers circulated a notice throughout Texas asking trail drivers not to bring their herds to Abilene.

Texas outfits were quite willing to comply. For by then the new railhead had moved to Ellsworth, 60 miles farther west. To guide the Texans, railroad workers had even marked a branch of the Chisholm Trail that led to Ellsworth. The branch split from the main Chisholm Trail near Wichita. The Kansas Pacific Railway Company (the new name for the Union Pacific in Kansas) also made it easier for the Texans. The company published a *Guide Map of the Great Texas Cattle Trail from Red River Crossing to the Old Reliable Kansas Pacific Railway* and distributed copies to Texas ranchers.

CATTLE DROVERS. NOTE LOCATION OF

K. P. DEAD LINE.

KANSAS PACIFIC RAILWAY,

THE OLD ESTABLISHED AND POPULAR

Texas Stock Route

GRAZING GOOD, WATER PLENTIFUL. SHIPPING FACILITIES PERFECT. YARDS FREE, RATES LOW.

2 Fast Stock Express Trains Daily from Ellis, Russell, Ellsworth, Brookville, Salina, Solomon and

ABILENE TO

KANSAS CITY AND LEAVENWORTH

Connecting with the following Roads:

ST. LOUIS, KANSAS CITY & NORTHERN; MISSOURI PACIFIC; CHICAGO, ALTON & ST. LOUIS; CHICAGO & ROCK ISLAND; TOLEDO, WABASH & WESTERN; HANNIBAL & ST. JOSEPH, AND KANSAS CITY, ST JOE & COUNCIL BLUFFS.

The only route by which Shippers have the choice of all the following Markets:

Denver, Colorado, Russell, Ellsworth, Leavenworth, Kansas City, Quincy, St. Louis and Chicago.

Drive to the KANSAS PACIFIC RAILWAY, and avoid hauls over new roads of 300 and 400 miles without transfer or rest.

Edmund S. Bowen,
Gen'l Supt
T. F. OAKES, Gen'l Freight Agt.,
KANSAS CITY, MO.

AND GOVERN YOURSELVES ACCORDINGLY.

A Kansas-Pacific announcement for the cattle (stock) trains, their routes, connections, and markets from Denver to Chicago.

The guide advertised the new trail and cited all the reasons why drovers should bring their herds to the railroad's stock pens in Ellsworth.

With the loss of trade, many Abilene businessmen loaded their goods in wagons and moved to Ellsworth, for a short time the reigning cow town, with saloons, dance hall girls, and gambling parlors. It had a sheriff, a marshal, and four deputies to see that people behaved—and a jail to put them in if they did not. While Ellsworth enjoyed its brief cattle boom, Abilene was all but forgotten.

Some of the buildings in Abilene, Kansas, which have been preserved to look much like they did in the late 1860s.

Meanwhile, the Atchison, Topeka & Santa Fe began to compete with the Kansas Pacific Railway Company for customers. In the early 1870s Santa Fe established railheads at several Kansas towns including Newton and Wichita, both on the Chisholm Trail south of Abilene.

The railroad reached Newton first. Almost overnight that tiny village grew into a cow town with over a thousand residents. Besides stockyards with six chutes to drive cattle into railroad stock cars, Newton had 27 saloons, eight gambling halls, three small hotels, six restaurants, and one doctor—but no bank, school, or church. For a single season, Newton had a reputation as the "wickedest town in Kansas." A year later, a spur line (branch) of the Santa Fe Railroad reached Wichita, farther south, and Texas cattlemen went there, instead. Newton's one season as a rip-roaring trail town was its last.

Although the Ellsworth branch of the Chisholm Trail began at Wichita, many Texas drovers loyal to the Kansas Pacific still trailed their herds past Wichita to Ellsworth. In time, however, they switched and began stopping at Wichita to ship their stock on the Santa Fe Railroad. By 1875 the boom for Ellsworth was over. Wichita was the new queen of the Kansas cattle towns.

Wichita and Wyatt Earp

By 1864 Wichita was the main cattle shipping town in Kansas. Like other rip-roaring cow towns before it, Wichita had its share of gambling house fistfights and free-for-all shooting sprees. To help keep the peace, the locals hired Wyatt Earp as deputy marshal. Before coming to Wichita, Wyatt Earp was a buffalo hunter, a stagecoach driver, and for a short time a police officer in Ellsworth.

Old Town Wichita, Kansas, has been preserved to look much as it appeared in the 1870s to 1880s.

FIVE

"Get Up an' Get It While It's Hot..."

Once the trail boss found a campground for the night, the cook—bumping along behind in his chuck wagon—reined in the mule team, unhitched and hobbled each animal (tied its forelegs so it could not wander), and started supper.

The cook was a vital member of the outfit, second only to the trail boss in authority and in the amount he was paid. The cook was usually older than the others in the outfit. Often he was an ex-cowboy who had to give up cowpunching after an injury.

A well-equipped chuck wagon was a necessity on the cattle drives.

On a drive, the cook worked hard. Each morning and afternoon he had to pack and move his portable "kitchen," and he still had to fix three meals every day. His stove was a fire built in a hole in the ground and he had no way to keep foods fresh. He had to prepare most meals with staples that did not spoil—flour, bacon, sugar, salt, dried and canned fruits, canned tomatoes, and coffee. Joking cowboys gave the plain foods fancy names: "Pecos strawberries" for boiled beans, "overland trout" for fried bacon. Outfits on northern trails often crossed trout-filled mountain streams and the crew could feast on the real thing. Sometimes farther south, too, cowboys camped near a stream and if they had time they might catch a fish for supper. They also shot game—turkeys, migrating ducks and geese, and sometimes a deer. Usually the men did not kill

Strong Coffee

Most cowboys drank a lot of coffee, and they liked it hot and strong. To make it, the cook dumped lots of ground coffee beans in the pot and boiled them for half an hour. He always kept a pot of coffee on hot coals through the night, for sleepy cowboys to drink before their turn at night watch.

The brand of coffee almost every trail cook used in the late 1800s was Arbuckle Brothers. The beans had been dipped in a mixture of egg and sugar that was supposed to keep in all of the coffee flavors. For a while, Arbuckle's included a stick of peppermint candy with every pound of coffee. The cook ground the coffee in a small hand-cranked coffee mill fastened to the chuck wagon. Sometimes he offered the candy cane to anyone who would grind the coffee for him and was swamped with eager volunteers.

"Come an' Get It!"

To call the men to breakfast the cook might shout "Roll out! Come an' get it! Come a-runnin'!" Or he might turn to poetry: "Bacon in the pan, coffee in the pot! Get up an' get it — Get it while it's hot!"

For the trail hands, seeing the same food day in and day out might prompt them to sing a ditty of their own: "Oh, it's bacon and beans 'most every day—I'd as soon be eatin' prairie hay."

animals from their own herd, since the meat would spoil without refrigeration. Occasionally they did kill a beef, or were given a quarter of beef by an outfit they met on the trail. Then, using all of the animal parts, the cook would make son-of-a-gun stew—a favorite with the cowboys.

In the spring the cook could liven up a meal with fresh onions, which grew wild in Indian Territory. In the summer, there were blackberries or wild plums to pick along the trail, and in the fall the men often gathered pecans. The only time cowboys on the trail saw eggs or fresh vegetables, however, was when they could offer a settler a calf from the herd in exchange for fresh produce. Besides eggs, what cowboys craved most were oysters and celery. These were the first foods many men ordered in a restaurant when they finally got to a town.

The earliest of the Texas cow herders had no cooks or chuck wagons. They ate whatever they could carry in their saddlebags that would keep for a week or longer, usually hard biscuits or cornbread and dried meat. After the Civil War, cowmen began using wagons on the trail. In 1866 Charles Goodnight designed a special food wagon he used

Charles Goodnight

on cattle drives and roundups, and in a few years nearly every outfit had a "Goodnight wagon." In the bed of the wagon the men stored their bedrolls, bags of flour, potatoes, dried fruit, and other supplies. A rawhide hammock that hung under the wagon provided more storage. To protect against sun and rain, a canvas cover could be stretched over wooden bows that arched over the wagon bed. Fastened somewhere on the wagon were a water barrel with a spout and a toolbox that held branding irons, an ax, a shovel, horse-shoeing equipment, and maybe a spare iron kettle or two.

At the back of the wagon in the chuck box were stored utensils, jugs of molasses and vinegar, and of course a big keg of fermenting sourdough batter for biscuits. Every time the cook took some of the fermenting batter he added more flour and salt and water to the keg. To make the biscuits he worked soda, lard, and more flour into the sourdough batter. He baked the biscuits in a Dutch oven—an iron baking pot with an iron lid—by setting the Dutch oven over hot coals and piling more hot coals on the lid.

Besides preparing meals for the outfit, the cook might be asked to give an occasional shave or haircut, sew on a shirt button, treat a cut, or remove a splinter. His first aid drawer in the chuck box held a few basic medications— calomel for a laxative, liniment to rub on sore muscles, and quinine for fever. Whisky might be included, due to a mistaken belief by some that it was a snakebite remedy.

Although the men liked to tease the cook, calling him "old woman," they tried hard to stay on his good side. They depended on those three meals a day. Trail bosses knew how important a good cook was and they picked their cooks with care, although sometimes a boss had to send a cook packing—that is, fire him. In one outfit on a northern trail the cook was sent packing because of where he parked his wagon. Instead of crossing a creek to set up camp, he camped on the near side. The trail boss was furious. He said that every old cowman knew enough always to camp at night on the far side of a creek. Then if a storm came, or someone broke an arm or leg or had some other sort of an accident, the outfit would already be across the stream.

Another outfit had a different problem with its cook. A blizzard with rain and sleet had scattered the herd in all directions. To collect the missing cattle the trail hands went without supper, a night's sleep, and breakfast. Then when the exhausted and hungry men finally got back to camp, they found no noon meal—and the cook hiding in his wagon under blankets. His excuse was that he couldn't build a fire because of the rain. The trail boss fired the cook and the cowboys started a fire and fixed their own dinner.

A hearty meal prepared by the trail cook was a welcome rest from a hard day's work.

SIX

The Western Trail
(Dodge Trail)

At the same time the railroad companies were hauling cattle East from Kansas, they were also encouraging easterners to come West. Their advertising campaigns and cheap train tickets lured many settlers to Kansas in the 1870s and 1880s. Cowboys called these newcomers "sodbusters," and resented the way they plowed under the prairie grasses that once provided fodder for cattle being trailed north. Like the settlers around Abilene, those in Wichita put up fences to keep Texas herds from crossing their land. Often a farmer plowed a single furrow around his field, and that was enough. According to Kansas laws, one plowed strip was considered a fence and anyone who crossed it might have to pay for damages to the property. Finally the Texas drovers were forced to find a shipping point farther west—and a trail to replace the old Chisholm that had taken them to Abilene, and later to Newton and Wichita.

The new railroad point many Texans chose was Dodge City. By the late 1870s, Dodge City had become the chief Kansas town for shipping cattle to midwestern feeders or slaughterhouses. Like Wichita, Dodge City was on the Santa Fe Railroad line—only much farther west. That meant that the drovers would be far away from settled areas, and not as likely to meet angry farmers or barbed wire fences.

By the 1870s the railroads had pushed to western Kansas and Colorado, where the Western Trail met them.

The trail to Dodge City was a branch of the Chisholm Trail. Beyond the Cimarron Crossing in Indian Territory the new branch angled northwest toward Dodge City. There was almost no water along this cut off. Many an outfit was grateful when rainstorms left enough water

Dodge City

Before Dodge City became a cattle shipping center its main trade items were buffalo meat and hides. First called Buffalo City, it was nothing but a few sod buildings where buffalo hunters gathered. By 1872, when the Santa Fe Railroad arrived, the tiny settlement had a general store, three dance halls, and six saloons, and was called Dodge City. It was named for nearby Fort Dodge, built seven years earlier to protect the Santa Fe Trail.

Dodge City was the last, longest-lived of the Kansas cow towns. Many called it "Hell on the Plains" and the "Wickedest Little City in America." Cowboys, buffalo hunters, gunfighters, and muleskinners thronged its streets where there was a saloon for every 20 citizens. Many strangers died in gunfights and were buried in Dodge's cemetery, called "boot hill" because so many of the unknowns were buried with their boots on.

Saloon keepers in Dodge City hired the marshal or sheriff to keep order. Wyatt Earp was an assistant city marshal of Dodge City before drifting to Tombstone, Arizona, during the silver boom. Bat Masterson—who had been buffalo hunter, scout, and gambler before being elected sheriff of Dodge City—was a gunman of quick draw and sure aim. He served two terms as sheriff of Dodge before he also moved to Tombstone, Arizona.

Dodge City, Kansas, as it appeared in 1878.

puddles for the thirsty animals to drink. As more Texans began trailing herds to Dodge City, many chose a new, more direct route west of the Chisholm cutoff.

This new route was first known as the Dodge Trail. Later it was called the Western Trail, or the Great Western Trail. Some northerners referred to it as the Texas Trail. As more Texans began to trail their herds beyond Kansas to Nebraska and Wyoming ranches, and to reservations in Dakota Territory and Montana, Dodge City became a favorite stopping place.

The Western Trail, like the Chisholm Trail, began in southern Texas, but after San Antonio, instead of going to Fort Worth, it angled north-west, following the Leon River to Fort Griffin. Like Dodge City, Fort Griffin had been a trading center for buffalo hides. By the time it became a stopover for cattle-

Buffalo hides piled high in a Dodge City, Kansas, hide yard.

men, professional hunters had managed to slaughter nearly every buffalo around. With most buffalo hunters gone, owners of Fort Griffin's general store and gambling houses were eager to offer supplies and games of chance to the cattle drivers.

To lure the cattlemen to Fort Griffin—rather than Fort Worth, 85 miles to the east—Fort Griffin merchants sent agents south to meet the drovers and persuade them to take the Western Trail. Most outfits did not need persuading. That route was the most direct to Dodge City anyway.

Beyond Fort Griffin, the Western Trail crossed the Red River at Doan's Crossing, named for a nearby store that

Jonathan Doan and his nephew, Corwin, started in 1878. Nearly every cattleman traveling on the Western Trail stopped at Doan's, the last settlement until they hit the Kansas line. The store sold whisky, Winchester rifles, cartridges, flour, bacon, blankets, Stetson hats, overalls, boots, and much more. Doan's had branding pens for the cattlemen to use, and was also a post office. Besides picking up canned goods, the men could collect their mail.

After Doan's Crossing the Western Trail led straight north through Indian Territory to Dodge City. For 15 years

An 1889 photo of Doan's Store at Doan's Crossing, Texas.

Dodge remained a bustling cattle town, with drovers trailing between 200,000 and 400,000 head of cattle there each year. Often there were so many cattle to be loaded onto stock cars that drovers had to wait their turns. One Texas outfit arrived at the Arkansas River outside Dodge with 3,000 head of cattle, only to discover 50 other herds already grazing in the river valley.

That night, there was a terrible storm, the worst that S. H. Woods, the outfit's young wrangler, had ever been through. He recalled seeing phosphorescence (fox fire) on the horses' ears and smelling sulfur. Then with a clap of thunder, a flash of lightning killed one of the lead steers and started a stampede. He said so many herds had run together that it was impossible to tell his outfit's cattle from others. When lightning flashed he could see thousands of cattle and hundreds of men all over the prairie. All the men could do was to wait for daybreak when all of the outfits got together and had a general roundup. It took them a week to get all the cattle into the correct herds.

The next important cattle town on the Western Trail after Dodge City was Ogallala, Nebraska, on the South Platte River. From Ogallala, branches led northwest to the Montana cow town of Miles City and straight north to Fort Buford, a military fort on the Missouri River in what is now northwestern North Dakota. Another branch from Ogallala followed the North Platte to Fort Laramie, Wyoming, and a fourth branch went west to Cheyenne, Wyoming, and then turned north to Fort Laramie and points beyond.

As soon as the Union Pacific Railroad reached Ogallala and Cheyenne in 1867 both towns became important shipping centers. By the late 1870s, both were bustling "wild and woolly" northern versions of Kansas cow towns to the south.

Most Texas cowboys who trailed herds north sold their horses and took the train back home. The Texas outfit S. H. Woods was with did not. Once the men reached northern Wyoming and delivered their herd—three months and 20 days after leaving the Red River—they were hired to trail a herd of Wyoming cattle to Glendive, Montana, a station on the Northern Pacific Railroad Line. There the men loaded the cattle onto rail cars and set off by train for Chicago. After they got rid of the herd they took a train home.

Trailing Texas cattle through Kansas had become very difficult by the 1880s. Severe quarantine laws kept the cattle out of many areas because they might carry disease, and farm fences hemmed in so much of the Western Trail that some Texas drovers had trouble finding open land where they could walk their herds to market. The busiest people in Dodge City were no longer cattle traders, but agents selling land in the thriving area to newcomers.

Texas Fever

For years, people did not know what caused Texas Fever. One theory was that the Texas soil was contaminated with a "poison" which the longhorns, who were immune, transported northward.

People finally realized that ticks carried north by the cattle caused the fever, but they still did not know how to get rid of the ticks—except to wait until they were killed by the winter frost. Only in the late 1880s, when Texans started sending cattle to market by train from their own state, instead of trailing them, did animal specialists discover that the ticks died when the cattle were dipped in a cleansing solution.

The Texas longhorn was immune to the Texas Fever.

During the era of the Long Drives, between 1860 and the early 1880s, Texans walked ten million cows to railheads in Kansas and Missouri. By the 1890s the days of the great Texas cattle drives were over. Most Texas cattle going north were shipped through Colorado. They were unloaded along the North Platte River and from there trailed to the Yellowstone, the Missouri, or the Milk River. Dodge City had survived as a shipping center longer than the other Kansas towns, but its turn as chief cow town was also coming to an end.

SEVEN

Troubles on
the Trail

"The wind commenced to blow and the rain began to fall;
Hit looked, by grab, like we was goin' to lose 'em all..."
from *The Old Chisholm Trail*, a cowboy song

B efore cowboys had trailed a herd far, they could expect trouble: bucking horses, violent storms, rustlers, midnight stampedes. Stampedes were the worst. Longhorns were naturally nervous with a keen sense of hearing and almost anything could cause them to panic. After a stampede one trail boss checked the ground where he had bedded his herd. It was pockmarked with huge gopher holes. A steer stepping into one of the holes had set off the stampede.

Usually a herd was more likely to stampede at the beginning of the drive, when the cattle were not used to the routine. Some cowboys believed that after two weeks without a stampede the danger was over, although this was not always the case. The animals were unpredictable. The skittering of a dry leaf might set off a herd and cowboys would spend the rest of the night rounding up cattle. Yet another time rolling thunder and flashing lightning might have no effect on a herd resting contentedly.

Stopping a herd of frightened, wild-eyed cattle from

stampeding was never easy, especially at night when most stampedes began. At a night guard's warning shouts, sleeping trail hands were out of their bedrolls and on their way to help as soon as they reached their horses. The fastest riders tried to catch the lead steers, then rein back to "worry them" into a trot—that is, slow the leaders. Other men rode at the side to keep the herd from splitting as they tried to turn the stampeders. In a night stampede, a good horse knew what to do without help from its rider. If cattle would not turn, cowboys fired their six-shooters into the ground close to the leaders' ears, or waved slickers in the stampeders' faces.

When the mounted cowboys finally threw the herd into a mill—got the cattle running in a large circle rather than straight ahead—the men rode around the circle to make it smaller and more compact. Eventually the milling cattle quieted and returned to their bed-ground, but for the rest of the night the cowboys kept watch to make sure the herd did not stampede again.

Cowboys at night awakening their relief watch.

Counting Cattle

After a stampede the trail hands counted the cattle to see if any were missing. To get an accurate count, since the number of lost animals could be as high as 50 or 100—or even more, the men would string out the herd. As the line of cattle passed slowly between two men on horseback, the men counted—sometimes using knots on their saddle strings. They kept track by the hundreds, one calling out to the other to be sure they agreed on the totals.

When daylight came, trail hands did their count and started a search if animals were missing. Cattle were not only killed or injured in stampedes, but after a long run—on a hot night, especially—they lost weight. A steer that weighed 50 pounds less than it had before cut into the owner's profits. Buyers wanted cattle that were fat and healthy, not stringy and gaunt.

River crossings presented serious problems when water overflowed the banks or wind created high waves. An outfit had to wait for the water to recede or the wind to die down before crossing. The animals swam across streams too deep to ford. The riders kept their place with the herd as they pointed the animals toward the opposite bank. The men tried to keep the cattle from milling in the water—going in circles—to prevent their being swept downstream and the cowboy and his horse with them. Many cowboys did not know how to swim. A man about to go under would try to grab the tail of a swimming steer but it did not always work. At nearly every crossing were the graves of cowboys who had fallen or were knocked off their mounts and drowned.

Both the Snake River in Idaho and the Red River between Texas and Indian Territory were prone to rampaging waters. At flood times, the Red River was nearly a mile wide, often forcing a dozen herds or more to wait on the Texas side for the water level to drop.

After one Texas outfit arrived to find the river too swollen to cross—and others waiting ahead of them—they pitched camp at nearby Panther Creek to wait their turn. Knowing it might take a while, the men killed a fat yearling (young cow or steer). That evening, the cook hung the meat from a rope between the chuck wagon and a small tree. At midnight a cowboy coming back from night watch saw a panther stretching on its hind legs to reach the beef. The cowboy opened fire with his .45 handgun. The panther ran into the woods, but the noise stampeded the cattle. The

A herd of Texas cattle crossing a stream as sundown approaches.

men spent the rest of that night and the next morning recovering the scattered herd.

Besides floods, wind, and high waves, a serious hazard at river crossings was quicksand. If cattle got bogged in the dangerous stuff, dragging them out with horses could take two or three days, and in some cases it was impossible ever to pull them free.

Even when river waters were calm, cattle sometimes balked at swimming across. One trail boss, who owned the herd he was trailing, had little experience crossing rivers with cattle. When his herd refused to swim across the Red River a more experienced trail hand pointed out that the animals were looking into the sun. He explained that you couldn't swim cattle across such a big stream in the morning if going east, or late of an afternoon if going west, for then the animals had the sun in their faces.

So the trail boss let the herd graze until one in the afternoon, when the sun was high enough for the cattle to see the other bank. Then the animals were quite willing to go across.

There were also times when a herd refused to cross a river for no reason. One herd would not cross a shallow stream no matter how much the trail hands tried to force them. Then another herd came by and the animals calmly crossed the stream. Immediately the first herd meekly followed their lead and went into the water.

Starting a stampede deliberately was also a way to get a reluctant herd across water. One outfit tried this and it worked. The stampeding cattle raced across the river without realizing it. On the other side, the cowboys quickly stopped the stampede.

EIGHT

Goodnight-
Loving Trail

While most Texas drovers followed the Shawnee or Chisholm Trails north, two ranchers on the frontier west of Fort Worth—Oliver Loving and Charles Goodnight—chose to combine their herds and trail their cattle west, to New Mexico.

In the spring of 1866, Goodnight put together a herd of a thousand head of cattle. He decided to go west instead of north to avoid the trouble with Missouri and Kansas quarantines, and also because he knew Colorado was a mining region with plenty of money. If he did not sell all of his herd right away he could hold them in Colorado where grazing was good.

It was while preparing for this drive that Goodnight designed the famous "Goodnight wagon" that became so

A version of the Goodnight chuck wagon is shown in this 1885 photo of a meal in the Texas-Oklahoma panhandle area.

popular with outfits all over the West. Goodnight bought a surplus army wagon with iron axles, then had a wood-worker rebuild the wagon adding a chuck box at the back end. The chuck box had a hinged lid that could be opened and brought down on a swinging leg to form a cook's work table. When closed, the lid would protect utensils and foods stored inside. Goodnight recalled how his efficient mother had always kept a jar of sourdough brewing so he made sure his chuck box had room for a keg of fermenting sourdough batter.

Before starting the drive west, Goodnight trailed his herd north to a settlement where he could buy supplies. On the way, he passed Oliver Loving's camp. Loving, who was gathering his cattle, asked about the drive. Despite

Charles Goodnight

Charles Goodnight came to Texas from Illinois with his family in 1845, when he was nine, riding horseback all the way on a little white-faced mare he called Blaze.

Before the Civil War began, Goodnight was a ranch hand and later had his own herd. During the war he was a scout and ranger in the Confederate Army. Goodnight had the "prairie smarts" that made him a good scout. He had perfect hearing and eyesight and a good sense of direction. He never got lost even without a map or compass. And he could always find water.

Goodnight could tell how recently a track was made by how dried up were the weeds that had been cut off by a horse's hoof. He could also tell if a hoofprint was made by a horse on the loose, a riderless horse being led, or a horse with a rider.

Loving's warnings about the difficulties of desert travel, Goodnight still insisted he was going. So Loving decided to go too.

The partners left Young County on June 6, 1866, with a combined herd of 2,000 cattle and 18 men. Loving was in charge. Goodnight acted as scout. He rode ahead to find water holes and grazing range, then doubled back to signal to the point riders the way the herd should go.

The route Charlie Goodnight followed was the old Butterfield Stage road west from Texas to the Pecos River. After crossing the Pecos, Goodnight planned to go north along the Pecos to New Mexico and then continue on to Colorado. Although a trail heading northwest from Texas to Colorado would have been shorter, it would have taken them through land controlled by Comanches and Kiowas. Goodnight felt the Pecos River route would take twice as long but at least they would arrive in Denver safely.

Starting west, Goodnight and Loving passed Buffalo Gap, a Butterfield Stage stop near the Texas town of Abilene. They crossed the North Concho River about 20 miles from the present town of San Angelo, then followed the Middle Concho west to its headwaters.

Here they stopped to fill canteens and water barrels, and to let the herd drink. This would be the last chance for water until they reached the Pecos River. The partners thought the distance to the Horsehead Crossing of the Pecos was about 100 miles—an almost impossibly long distance for cattle to go without water. Still, they were going to try. They let the herd drink until the animals could suck up no more. When the sun was low in the sky, they started west.

Oliver Loving

The Goodnight-Loving Trail was developed as an easier route to the westernmost railheads in Colorado.

They kept the cattle moving until late, but when the men finally bedded the animals down, the cattle would not stay down. It took the whole outfit to keep them from wandering off. Goodnight and Loving decided that since the cattle were wasting their energy walking in circles, they might as well be walking toward the Pecos River. From then on, the outfit pushed on both day and night without rest.

By the third day, men and animals were miserable. The trail hands could scarcely keep from dozing off. Some even tried rubbing tobacco juice on their eyelids to stay awake. The weary and parched cattle bawled and moaned for water as they stumbled along. The weaker ones fell to the ground, unable to go on.

Suddenly on the evening of the third day, a gentle breeze blew. As soon as the cattle smelled the cool, damp air they became wild for water and made a frantic stampede toward the river, 12 miles away. A few cattle drank poisonous water from alkali pools near the river and died. Many were lost when they bolted over a steep riverbank, were trapped, and could not climb back up. Others got bogged down in the quicksand.

At that crossing of the Pecos, Goodnight and Loving lost 100 animals. With the rest of the herd they continued northwest through the desolate Pecos valley—home to many rattlesnakes but few other living things. Goodnight called the Pecos "the graveyard of the cowman's hopes."

The outfit followed the winding Pecos up through New

Horsehead Crossing

The Horsehead Crossing of the Pecos River was on the main Comanche trail from the Great Plains to Chihuahua in northern Mexico. According to a legend, the crossing got its name because of all the horse skulls there. The Comanches rode their horses so hard across the arid lands to reach the river that the desperately thirsty animals drank too much briny Pecos water and most of them died.

Mexico. When they reached Fort Sumner, the partners cut out 800 head of stock cattle, which Loving would take on north to Colorado. Then they sold what was left to the fort's agent for $12,000 in gold coins, a good profit.

Loving then headed north. With three men, Goodnight started back to Texas where he wanted to collect another herd to trail west before winter set in. The four men rode saddle mules, but each led a horse that he could switch to in case of attack. Goodnight packed the gold coins with the provisions on a pack mule.

On their 700-mile saddle trip back to Texas, the men slept by day and traveled at night. One night something scared the pack mule and it bolted ahead. By the time the men found it the load had fallen off. They searched frantically in the dark. At last they found the money, but no food except a slab of bacon.

In the Texas desert a day or two later they met Rich Coffee, an old settler on his way to Utah to buy a load of salt. In his wagon were watermelons which he planned to sell along the way to Mexican traders. Rich Coffee happily shared his melons with the hungry Texans, and also gave them enough provisions to get the rest of the way home.

Once back in Taylor County, Goodnight gathered together a herd to drive west over the new trail he and Loving had established. The trail that Loving followed from Fort Sumner and Denver, and the trail Goodnight later took from Denver to Cheyenne, also became parts of what soon came to be known as the Goodnight-Loving Trail.

NINE

Oregon
Cattle Trail

Oregonians were trailing cattle to some parts of Wyoming and Montana by the early 1870s. In 1876, the Sioux and the Cheyenne signed a treaty that opened to settlers many more acres of grassland east of the Rockies. Some of the "settlers" who rushed to start ranches were wealthy businessmen—many of them from England, Scotland, and France. They bought cattle from both Texas and Oregon, then often hired managers to run the ranches.

The Oregon cattle that were trailed east were descendants of the milk cows that pioneers brought west when they first settled in the Willamette Valley in the mid-1800s. The Oregon stock with their shorter horns were more docile than the Texas longhorns.

One of the "Cattle Kings of the Northwest," G. A. Searight, had a ranch near Cheyenne. He hired trail boss Andy Carr and 25 experienced cattle drivers to travel to Oregon and bring back 5,000 cattle for his ranch. Most of the cowboys were Texans who had come north on cattle drives and decided to stay. On March 4, 1879, the *Cheyenne Sun* newspaper reported that the young men left by train the afternoon before amid cheers and shouts of townspeople who gathered at the Union Pacific depot to see them off.

The cowboys took horses, wagons, stores, saddles, and

baggage by train to Ogden, a popular outfitting center in northern Utah. There they bought provisions and then headed overland toward Baker City in eastern Oregon. Their journey by way of Utah and Idaho took about six weeks. Before starting their long trip back to Wyoming the men spent another three weeks gathering their herd and getting the cattle road-branded.

For the next dozen years, other outfits like Andy Carr's trailed cattle east from Oregon. Some cowboys, like Carr, went to Baker City by way of Ogden. Others took the train all the way to San Francisco, where they caught a boat to Portland, Oregon, and then continued another 80 miles up the Columbia River to The Dalles. From there they went overland to Baker City to assemble the wagons and horses they would need.

The goal of some Oregon cattle drives was this stockyard in Cody, Wyoming, where cattle could be held until shipped farther east.

Some western cowhands who went to Oregon brought their wagons and a small number of horses all the way from their ranches. When they finally arrived in Baker City they bought more horses, and spent time breaking them in. In the north, the string of horses that accompanied a drive was often called cavvy rather than remuda. *Cavvy* came from caballo, the Spanish word for horse.

Cattlemen from all parts of Washington and Oregon brought animals to sell in Baker City. Trailing the cattle east from Baker required following winding paths through the Rocky Mountains—much slower going than along the Chisholm Trail over prairie flatlands. Cowboys following the Oregon Cattle Trail could travel about eight or ten miles in a day. Most outfits arrived at their destination east of the Rockies in seven months if all the cattle were steers

The Oregon Trail was developed in the 1880s to drive cattle from the Far West to better markets in the Midwest and the East.

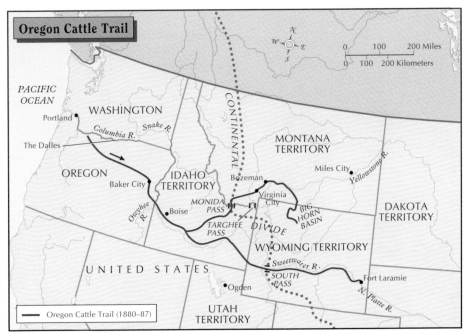

(castrated bulls). Trailing a mixed herd (one with cows and calves as well as steers) took longer.

In a large mixed herd, calves were born every day or night. In most cases they were killed right away, especially if the mother cows were too thin and weak to care for them. Along the part of the trail by Camas Creek in eastern Idaho, homelands of the Bannock and the Shoshone, the people were happy to claim for food the calves the cowboys had to leave behind.

One outfit going east on the Oregon Cattle Trail tried to keep most of the newborn calves whose mothers were healthy. The trail hands built a pen in the back of the wagon carrying the bedrolls so they could haul three or four newborns at a time. At night when the cattle were bedded, the men turned the calves back to their mothers. Then they put the babies back in the wagon for the morning's drive. At noon they staked out the calves, and the mothers came by and suckled their youngsters. After two or three days these calves were old enough to walk beside their mothers and other newborns took their places in the wagon.

Troubles began for trail drivers at the very start of the Oregon Cattle Trail when herds had to cross the Snake River on the Oregon-Idaho border. The banks of the Snake were so steep that drovers found few breaks where their animals could get down to the water. One of the best places to cross the Snake was just above the mouth of the Owyhee River. Here someone built a corral and chute at the edge of the Snake. Cattle could be kept in the corral, then herded through the chute to make sure they entered the river at the right place.

If crossing the Snake, the trail drivers always had to do it while water was still low, in late winter or early spring. By mid-May the river rose to become a raging torrent too

$200,000 in a Box

Texas cowhand James Dahlman was twenty-five and working on a ranch near Sidney, Nebraska, when he and several other cowhands went to Oregon with their boss (the ranch owner) to bring back 20,000 head of cattle. The stock was to be divided into several herds to be delivered to the boss's two ranches—the N-Bar in Nebraska and the N-Bar in Montana.

Like other cowmen at the time, the men got to Baker by a combination of rides on stagecoaches and trains. In their case, they had a special problem. Since bank checks were not commonly used to pay for purchases, the boss was carrying the money for his cattle in a cardboard shoe box wrapped with heavy string. The box contained between $200,000 and $300,000 in bills. Dahlman, his boss, and the boss's male secretary were the only three in the group who knew what was in the box.

"I remember that shoe box mighty well!" Dahlman said later. "The sign on it stated that the shoes were made in St. Louis. Whenever we went into an eating house all through that trip, one of us would set the box down

dangerous to cross. Afternoon was the best time of day to ford the Snake. Then, the sun was behind the cattle. In the morning the sun was in their eyes and sunlight reflected on the river waves, frightening the animals.

Once in Idaho the Oregon Cattle Trail continued to Boise, one of the few settlements along the way for buying provisions. For about 50 miles beyond Boise the trail continued along a high grassy plateau north of the Snake. In an area of strange lava formations known as the Lava Beds, trail bosses had to make a choice. They could go on for 45 miles with plenty of grass but no water, or take a longer detour with little grass but some water. In the hot summer, many took the longer way, since cattle could do without

on the counter, in a sort of offhand manner, as though we were just carrying an extra pair of shoes or a few sandwiches, or maybe a clean shirt."

Despite Dahlman's worries along the way, they arrived safely in Baker City with the shoe box, and the money was soon used up buying the 20,000 head of stock, 500 horses, wagons, and provisions.

Dahlman was put in charge of a herd of 2,800 cattle going to the Nebraska ranch. He got them as far as South Pass in eastern Nebraska when a courier met him to say that prairie fires to the east had destroyed the feed. Dahlman knew that even if he did not run up against the fire itself, there would be nothing for his cattle to eat. So instead of continuing east, he turned north toward Montana.

When Jim Dahlman finally arrived at the Montana ranch, near Miles City, he had been on the trail six months. After all the herds were counted, the boss found that Dahlman had lost the fewest cattle along the way of any of the foremen, and so he rewarded him with a pearl-handled gun, a holster, and a knife.

food for a couple of days but they had to have water.

In eastern Idaho the Snake River curves north, and outfits had to cross it a second time. This time, they could use the bridge at Eagle Rock (near present-day Idaho Falls). Since the bridge toll was twenty-five cents a head, however, many outfits decided to take their chances and make their crossing farther south, near the town of Blackfoot.

Just after this second Snake River crossing, the Oregon Cattle Trail divided into two trails. The Southern Trail went east into Wyoming, following the Lander cutoff of the old Oregon Trail. At South Pass, this trail crossed the Continental Divide that separates streams flowing west from those flowing east. At a settlement just past South

Pass were a post office and stores where people could buy food and supplies. From here the Southern Trail followed along Wyoming's Sweetwater and then North Platte Rivers.

While the Southern Trail continued more or less straight east, the Northern Trail angled north and east. Near Idaho's eastern border it split, with one branch crossing the Continental Divide at Monida Pass (6,870 feet high) and the other branch crossing the divide at the Targhee Pass (7,072 feet high). In Montana these two northern trails divided several more times. One branch dipped south to the Big Horn Basin in northwestern Wyoming. Another continued to Miles City on the Yellowstone River in eastern Montana, and then into the Dakotas. Other branches reached into other parts of Montana.

By 1890, Oregon was running out of cattle to sell to easterners. After that, fewer herds were trailed east and more cattle were kept in the Pacific Northwest to feed people in the cities and towns of Washington and Oregon.

The Targhee Pass today, on U.S. Highway 20, at the border of Montana and Idaho.

TEN

Women on the Trail

The world of the cowboy, especially on the cattle drives north, was almost completely a man's world. Once in a while, though, women chose to go along. In Mason County in central Texas the wife of D. M. (Doc) Barton joined her husband when he started north with 500 long-horns. Mrs. Barton rode a cow pony and worked as a trail hand on the drive. The Barton's baby rode in the chuck wagon with the cook. When the chuck wagon got stuck in the mud one time, Native Americans passing by helped pull it out and a grateful Mrs. Barton rewarded them with a jar of cookies.

Mrs. George W. Gluck, a rancher's wife from Nueces County in central Texas, went north with her husband in the spring of 1871 when he trailed a herd of 1,000 steers to Kansas. Mrs. Gluck and her three children (aged seven, five, and two) rode in a small wagon drawn by two ponies. Besides camping gear and bedding, she brought along a spyglass and her shotgun.

When the group reached the Red River, the river was on a rampage and the water was high and rough. Mrs. Gluck and her husband rode across together on one horse, while trail hands on horses carried the children. To get the wagon over, the men tied cottonwood logs on each side so it would float. Then the ponies pulled it as they swam across.

In Indian Territory a large band of rustlers confronted the Texans demanding a part of the herd. Mrs. Gluck, who stayed in the wagon helping load the guns, is reported to have told the trail hands: "If any one of you boys doesn't want to fight, come here and drive the hack and give me your gun." Meanwhile, Mr. Gluck faced the rustlers, gun in hand, and refused their demand. Although the rustlers far outnumbered the Texans, they apparently thought better of their plan, wheeled around, and rode off.

Another rancher's wife, Amanda Burks, went on an early drive north when her husband and another rancher named Clark trailed their herds to Kansas. On the way, the two men kept the herds a few miles apart. Mrs. Burks drove a little buggy drawn by "two good brown ponies." She did not worry when she got tired, for the horses did not seem to need a driver. They simply followed the slow-moving herd unguided. Meanwhile, Mrs. Burks found a comfortable position, fastened the lines, and took a little nap.

It was rare to see a woman with a string of horses on the trail.

At night, Mrs. Burks stayed alone in her own tent away from the camp. One afternoon she was alone in camp when two men came up and began throwing rocks at the grazing cattle. She told them to stop or they would start a stampede. They told her that was what they were trying to do. Fortunately, a couple of trail hands returned to camp and scared off the would-be rustlers.

A few days later both the Burks and Clark herds did stampede. No one was sure of the cause, but it took the men almost a week to gather the cattle and separate them into the right herds. Afterward the trail hands were so tired that the tenderfoot of the outfit, young Branch Isbell, lay down and fell asleep. He slept so soundly that he did not hear the others when they broke camp and left. It was evening before he finally caught up with them again.

On that drive, Mrs. Burks had to cope with all kinds of disasters. She endured electrical storms and hailstorms where she said the lightning seemed to settle on the ground and "creep along like something alive." She also survived several prairie fires. The first fire ran everyone out of camp before breakfast. They escaped by fleeing to a "burn"—a part of the plain that had been burned before. Another time, as Mrs. Burks was starting a cooking fire, the match she struck ignited the dry grass. That fire blazed higher than a house, and went straight ahead for 50 miles or more. A third fire startled the group as they camped along a creek. The men barely had time to break up camp and get themselves and their cattle safely to a burn.

According to Mrs. Burks, many of the prairie fires were started by squatters who wanted to keep strangers away from the land. The squatters—settlers who still did not have title to their land—would plow a safety boundary around their stake and then set fire to the grass outside.

While women were not usually permitted on the trail, they were often needed on the ranch to brand cattle (as shown here), or to set off on horseback to locate stray cattle, to mend broken fences, and to inspect water holes.

Veteran cowboy Samuel Dunn Houston told of a woman who joined a cattle drive on her own and worked as a trail hand. She was Willie Matthews of Caldwell, Kansas. Her father had been a trail driver and he had often told her how exciting life was on the trail. When Willie was ten, she made up her mind that when she was older she would go up the trail herself—even if she had to run away from home to do it.

In 1888, when she was nineteen, Willie read in the paper about the big cattle herds passing through Clayton, New Mexico, that spring. Here was her chance at last! She borrowed her brother's suit and boots and saddled her pony. She told her brother she was leaving for a while and asked him to tell their father not to worry because she would be back in a week or so.

It took Willie four days to ride to Clayton. When she arrived, she asked at the livery stable about jobs. Someone remembered that Sam Dunn Houston had just arrived in town and needed a trail hand. She and Houston met. He decided this "kid"—who, he thought, was a boy—would do just fine as a wrangler. Although slight of build and not very strong, Willie seemed to be good-natured and "didn't use any cuss words or tobacco."

Willie Matthews did her job well, working through stormy nights with the rest of the hands to watch over the herd until the danger passed. About a week later, the outfit reached Hugo, Colorado, on the railroad line near the Wyoming border. Here Willie told Houston she was homesick and wanted to quit. He let her go, but around sundown that same day as he and his trail hands were sitting around in camp she returned.

This time, Willie wore a dress with a long skirt. Houston couldn't imagine why a woman would be coming on foot to a cow camp. When he found out this was the "kid" who had been his wrangler, Houston asked her to explain. Willie sat on a tomato box the cook brought out for a chair and told the men her story. She finished by saying how much she had enjoyed the trip and that now she was going home on the 11:20 train from Hugo. Houston left one man to guard the herd and he and the rest of the outfit went to the train station to see her off.

A Lasting Heritage

Driving through the western plains and prairies today, with their many roads and fences and towns, it is hard to imagine that at one time a wide belt of grassland extended from southern Texas to the Canadian border. Cowboys trailing their herds could ride in the same direction for hours and hours—or even days—with nothing blocking their way but an occasional river or stream to cross.

Although many western cattle trails have been plowed under and forgotten, it is still possible to follow routes that—in places, at least—are very close to the original trails.

The total span of the cattle drives was short, less than 25 years, and the total number of cowboys who took part fairly small—possibly 35,000. But few events in American history have had such a powerful effect on American folklore and literature and on the imaginations of people all over the world.

Tallgrass Prairie in Preserve, Oklahoma, is typical of much of the country cattle trails crossed.

88

Glossary

artillery Slang for a cowboy's "six-shooter," a revolver that would fire six shots without reloading.

brand Mark burned on the side of a cow to indicate ownership.

buckaroo Another word for cowboy, from Spanish *vaquero* (skilled horseman).

bust Train a horse so it can be ridden with a saddle and bridle.

cavvy Another name for remuda, the string of horses that accompanies a cattle drive (from *caballo*, Spanish for horse).

Conestoga wagon A style of covered wagon used to carry freight.

dogie Orphan calf whose mother was dead or missing.

drag riders Inexperienced, or "green," cowboys who rode at the rear of the herd being trailed, just behind the drags.

drags Trailed cattle too weak or lame to keep up; stragglers.

drover One who drives animals to market.

earmark Nick at the upper or lower edge of cow's or steer's ear to identify the owner; a triangular piece may be nipped from the tip, or the bottom of the ear cut squarely across.

feeders Persons who buy animals to fatten up in their stockyards for later sale.

flank riders On the trail, cowboys riding at either side of the herd, farther back than the swing riders.

freighter A mule driver in charge of a train of mules hauling goods, also known as a muleskinner.

hog-tie To tie all four feet of an animal together.

homestead 160 acres of public land given under the Homestead Act of 1862 to householders who would settle and farm it for five years.

jingle bob Cow's earmark in which the flappy part is deeply split.

lariat Twisted hemp (plant fiber) rope which Texans looped to catch a steer on the run; from the Spanish *la reata* (braided rawhide rope).

maverick Unbranded or orphaned animal. "To maverick" meant to mark and brand a stray range animal. Later it came to mean any person who is independent and unattached to a particular cause — especially a political party.

mixed herd One with cows and calves as well as steers.

mustang Wild horse of the American plains, broken to the saddle.

nooning Stopping for a midday meal; a pioneer and cowboy term.

packing house Firm that slaughters, processes, and packs livestock into meat and meat products.

point riders On the trail, cowboys riding beside the lead steers to keep them heading in the right direction.

Prince Albert coat A man's long, double-breasted, knee-length coat, named for Prince Albert Edward, later King Edward VII of England.

quicksand Mixture of loose sand and water that can engulf anything resting on its surface.

railhead The point to which rails have been laid on an unfinished railroad.

remuda Extra saddle horses for each cowboy, herded together when away from the ranch and watched over by the wrangler.

road brand Additional brand given to cattle to be trailed together.

sodbusters Newcomers to Kansas in the 1870s and 1880s who plowed under the prairie grasses that once provided fodder for cattle being trailed north.

sourdough Sour fermented dough used as leaven (yeast) in making bread.

stock cars Railroad cars in which animals were hauled.

stock cattle Cattle used for breeding, to start new herds.

swing riders On the trail, cowboys riding farther back, where the herd began to spread wider.

"Texas cows" Breed of cattle with especially long, curved horns; also called Texas longhorns.

Texas fever Common name for a fatal cow's disease caused by ticks.

wrangler Cowboy in charge of the remuda.

Further Reading

Baker, Charlotte. *Trails North—Stories of Texas Yesterdays*. Eakin-Sunbelt, 1991

Folsom, Franklin. *Black Cowboy: The Life and Legend of George McJunkin*. R. Rinehart, 1992

Greenlaw, M. Jean. *Ranch Dressing: The Story of Western Wear*. Dutton, 1993

Katz, William L. *The Black West*. Open Hand Publishing, 1986

Landau, Elaine. *Cowboys*. Franklin Watts, 1990

Lightfoot, D.J. *Trail Fever: The Life of a Texas Cowboy*. Lothrop, Lee, & Shepard, 1992

Marrin, Albert. *Cowboys, Indians, and Gunfighters: The Story of the Cattle Kingdom*. Macmillan, 1993

Miller, Brandon M. *Buffalo Gals, Women of the Old West*. Lerner, 1993

Murdoch, David H. *Cowboy*. Knopf, 1993

Myres, Sandra L. *Westering Women and the Frontier Experience, 1800-1915*. University of New Mexico Press, 1982

Seidman, Laurence I. *Once in the Saddle: The Cowboy's Frontier 1866-1896.* Facts on File, 1990

Shapely, R. *Boomtowns.* Rourke, 1990

Stewart, Gail B. *Cowboys in the Old West.* Lucent Books, 1995

Bibliography

* Indicates book of special interest to young adult readers

*Abbott, E.C. ("Teddy Blue") and Smith, Helena Huntington. *We Pointed Them North*, New York: Farrar & Rinehart, Inc., 1939; reprinted by University of Oklahoma Press, 1966.

*Adams, Andy. *The Log of a Cowboy: A Narrative of the Old Trail Days*, Boston: Houghton Mifflin Company, 1903.

Beckstead, James H. *Cowboying*, Salt Lake City: University of Utah Press, 1991.

*Brown, Dee. *Trail Driving Days*, New York: Charles Scribner's Sons, 1952.

*Dobie, J.Frank. *Cow People*, Boston: Little, Brown & Co., 1964.

*————*The Longhorns*, Boston: Little, Brown & Co., 1941.

*Durham, Philip D. and Jones, Everett L. *The Adventures of the Negro Cowboys*, New York: Dodd-Mead, 1965.

Dykstra, Robert R. *The Cattle Towns*, New York: Alfred A. Knopf, 1968.

*Forbis, William H. *The Cowboys* ("The Old West" series), Alexandria, Virginia: Time-Life books, 1973.

Gard, Wayne. *The Chisholm Trail*, Norman: University of Oklahoma Press, 1954.

Haley, J. Evetts. *Charles Goodnight, Cowman & Plainsman*, Norman: University of Oklahoma Press, 1949.

Hollon, W. Eugene. *The Southwest: Old and New*, New York: Alfred A. Knopf, 1961.

Hunter, *The Trail Drivers of Texas, vol.1 and 2*, New York: Argosy-Antiquarian Ltd., 1963.

*Monaghan, Jay. *The Book of the American West*, New York: Bonanza Books, 1963.

*Place, Marian T. *American Cattle Trails East & West*, Holt, Rinehart & Winston, 1967.

Rollinson, John K. *Wyoming Cattle Trails (History of the Migration of Oregon-raised Herds to Mid-Western Markets)*, Caldwell, Idaho: The Caxton Printers, Ltd., 1948.

*Sandler, Martin W. *Cowboys: A Library of Congress Book*, New York: Harper-Collins, 1994.

Worcester, Don. *The Chisholm Trail: High Road of the Cattle Kingdom*, Lincoln and London: University of Nebraska Press, 1980.

Index

Note: Page numbers in italics indicate maps; numbers in bold indicate illustrations.